T0362953

BORN IN 1962?

WHAT ELSE HAPPENED?

RON WILLIAMS

AUSTRALIAN SOCIAL HISTORY

BOOK 24 IN A SERIES OF 35

FROM 1939 to 1973

BOOM, BOOM BABY, BOOM

BORN IN 1962? WHAT ELSE HAPPENED?

Published by Boom Books
Wickham, NSW, Australia
Web: www.boombooks.biz
Email: email@boombooks.biz

© Ron Williams 2013. This edition 2023.
A single chapter or part thereof may be copied and reproduced without permission, provided that the Author, Title, and Web Site are acknowledged.

Creator: Williams, Ron, 1934- author.

Title: Born in 1962? : what else happened?

ISBN: 9780645182613

Subjects:Australia--History--Miscellanea--20th century.

Some Letters used in this text may still be in copyright. Every reasonable effort has been made to locate the writers. If any persons or their estates can establish authorship, and want to discuss copyright, please contact the author at email@boombooks.biz

Cover image: National Archives of Australia

A1200, 30451968 AFS scholar and host

A12111, 7501945 Elephant trainer

A1501 8918186 Children at play

A1200 30672486 Whaling industry

TABLE OF CONTENTS

SOME IMPORTANT PEOPLE AND EVENTS

Queen of England	Elizabeth II
Prime Minister of Oz	Robert Menzies
Leader of Opposition	Arthur Calwell
Governor General	Viscount De L'Isle
The Pope	Pius XXIII
US President	John F Kennedy
PM of Britain	Harold Macmillan

Winner of Ashes:

1961	Australia 2 - 1
1962-63	Drawn 1 - 1
1964	Australia 1 - 0

Melbourne Cup Winners:

1961	Lord Fury
1962	Even Stevens
1963	Gatum Gatum

Academy Awards

Best Actor	Maximillian Schell
Best Actress	Sophia Loren
Best Movie	West Side Story

JANUARY NEWS ITEMS

The Highlands Society of NSW will today (Jan 1st) hold a gathering that will include Scottish country dancing, highland dancing, cycling, women's athletics, a tug o' war, a pipe bands contest, a corps of drums contest, a drum-majors contest, a massed band parade, and chariot racing.

The Prime Minister, Bob Menzies, broadcast a ho-hum New Year's message. "The Government will carry on its job of maintaining a stable economy, along with the development of our natural resources, so that the riches of our country may be enhanced to the true benefit of all.".

The Leader of the Opposition, Arthur Calwell, uttered more platitudes, and added that "we must be determined enough to believe that, through the UN, we will find ways to prevent wars and to overcome those problems which have vexed us, and seem to defy solution."

Cricket Test Captain, Richie Benaud, was granted an O.B.E. by the Queen in the New Year's Honours List.

The uniform rail gauge link between Sydney and Melbourne will be opened January 2nd. No longer will passengers be required to change trains at Albury. This will be especially appreciated by over-night travelers, who previously had been moved from their beds at Albury at about mid-night. Freight trains will pass through Albury without re-loading.

wsaThe price of a bride in the Eastern Highlands of New Guinea was now between 200 and 300 Pounds. In other nearby Islands, New Britain and New Ireland, the price was only 10 Pounds. In Port Moresby this week, 53 worried Local Government Councils met to establish a fair-average price.

Quote from fiery Frank Sinatra: "Some guys have big mouths, but I have big fists."

After the War, NSW (and other States) established a Housing Commission to build houses to ease the shortage....

The American Medical Association warned that the new dance craze, The Twist, is a source of dislocated joints, slipped discs, sacroiliac damage or muscle sprains. This was especially so for persons over 40 years of age.

Sydney police arrested 117 men and women on gaming charges in a two-storey building in Leichardt. Those arrested had been gambling on two-up, bacarrat, and poker. About 25 men escaped by climbing down drainpipes. A similar raid on the same premises a week ago netted 49 gamblers. Such raids were common in all cities across Australia, presumably because of no venues for legal gambling.

The Housing Commission of NSW reported that its waiting list now stands at 35,000. Housing Commission homes were built on large estates, and were of standard designs, but offered cheaper accommodation than building through private builders. The shortage of modern houses in Australia is very severe.

OUR LOCAL POLITICAL SCENE

The Federal election in 1961 had been a tame affair. Neither Party had any new policies that they were game enough to tell the electorate about, and both parties stood on their record. What they could hope to gain from this was anyone's guess. Menzies obviously hoped that people would remember that he had been in office for 10 years, and that the nation had been prosperous and stable and at peace for all that time.

On the other hand, what voters did remember was that Menzies, over the last year, had introduced a credit squeeze to the nation. As usual, this cut off a lot of imports that people wanted, forced up prices, made jobs a bit harder to get, reduced the number of home loans for housing, and heaps more. By the time the elections came, the voters had seen enough, and quite a few decided to throw out Menzies, and take a risk with Labour.

The Opposition, the Labour Party, led by Arthur Calwell, had been in self-destruct mode for several years. Calwell was a politician who seemed to be biting at the heels of the Government at all times, and to be obsessed with scoring political points **rather than formulating policies**.

His Party was faction-ridden, with Left wings and Right wings, and Catholic break-away groups, and so-called Democrats within or about. The only light on the horizon was a young, new, Deputy Leader called Gough Whitlam, but because he was smooth and educated, it would take him a long time to be heard among the "old die-hards in their smoke-filled back-rooms".

THE INTERNATIONAL SCENE

The Second World War had brought a new vision to the hundred nations who were under colonial rule. As the Germans or Japanese were being trundled out, these nations became anxious to ensure that the old colonial powers, Britain, the Dutch, the French and the Portugese did not get back to their pre-War status. They could see a new world, free from colonial oversight, that gave them equal status in all things. Along with this, in many countries, coloured races were also demanding equality. In the USA, in South Africa, and a dozen other nations, violent and non-violent demands for equality were reverberating.

By 1962, there were dozens of nations in various stages of turmoil over these two issues, and some of them were even in civil war or various stages on anarchy. We will keep an eye on them as we go, always conscious that they had a lesson for Australia, but conscious that we were lucky enough to be far removed from their violence. Though, we did have to keep in mind that not too far away, Indonesia was forming itself into a new nation, and that the Dutch-held West New Guinea would possibly be the scene of violent confrontation soon. Also, though we were slow to recognise it, we had our own sizeable black population, and while they were generally quiescent at the moment, maybe the examples overseas would encourage some similar actions here.

Ongoing with these two great movements, was an idealogical split that pitched into both issues. That was Communism versus Capitalism, of Russia versus America, of good versus evil, or was it evil versus good. Both countries were everywhere spreading the idea that **its** economic system was the only one that would save the world, that **its** bombs were better that any other, that **its** armies could walk over anyone anywhere at any time, and that on top of that, they were really good guys. It was all so silly, but to struggling groups wanting to be free from something, the offers of military help, and financial help, were very attractive.

Australians had largely out-grown this nonsense. Over the last decade and more, they had been so often threatened with world wars, by the dropping of any number of bombs, by military conflicts here and there, that they were now generally took little notice. The Great Powers were highly tense about the fate of West Berlin. Ho Hum. The Russians were promising military aid to Indonesia. Ho Hum. The Americans had discovered a spy ring right in the centre of the Pentagon. More Ho, More Hum. Most overseas scare events, and there were so many of them, were relegated to Page Three of our Newspapers, and only got about six column-inches.

COLONISTS OUT OF NEW GUINEA?

West New Guinea (West Irian) was now a bone of contention between the embryonic State of Indonesia, and the very old colonial power of Holland. The Dutch had held some of the islands on Indonesia for up to four centuries, and had poured a lot of capital, manpower, and intelligent thought into developing them into a worthwhile trading nation. After the Japanese had captured its many hundreds of islands, and it had been liberated, it wanted to keep its liberty, and so over the next 15 years, the Dutch were slowly and reluctantly removed from the scene. West Irian was, in 1962, one small part of the old colony still under Dutch control, and the Indonesians now thought that it was time to change that.

The situation now was that in Indonesia, the Prime Minister, Dr Soekarno, was making aggressive growling noises and marshalling armed forces near West Irian. The Dutch were holding up their hands saying we want to talk about this. Australia had no direct interest in the dispute that was developing. We did have a UN mandate over **eastern** New Guinea, so we could interpose under the guise of neighbours, but we had no further legal involvement. That did not stop us from fiddling at the edges, and we were clearly supporting the Dutch. Just now we had said that we would become involved in a war only if our Great Friends, Britain and the US, were also involved. This was a clever thing to say, because neither of those Great Friends, despite their rhetoric, had any intention of getting involved in any hostilities.

Public opinion was very vocal, and the Papers and pulpits and Parliaments were full of good advice to any one who would listen. There were two dozen different types of arguments, and I will present just a few of them below.

Letters, A MacDonald. Would it not be better for our future security's sake not to raise objections when New Guinea is invaded, as it will be, but rather offer Indonesia special aid for the advancement of the Papuans? It would be sacrificing no principle to show ourselves to be the friend of both the Indonesians and the Papuans at the same time.

Out of the legal complexity of Indonesia's revolution, we find that the claim to West New Guinea rests on the fact that the modern State of Indonesia is considered the successor of the Netherlands East Indies, and therefore is rightful possessor of all the territories formerly ruled by the Dutch, including West New Guinea.

In the short run, it is most important to keep Indonesia's goodwill and mind our own business by developing a strong Eastern New Guinea. In the long run, we should hope to create and keep friendly relations with a group of stable, peaceful nations to our north on a basis of equality and cooperation. For the time being, it would be better for us to have a friendly Indonesia owning West New Guinea rather than a vengeful, frustrated enemy only a few hours from Darwin.

Letters, L Shaw. Dr Soekarno regards West New Guinea as belonging rightfully to Indonesia, although geographically and racially such a claim is nonsense.

And if the western part of an island is so regarded, what about the rest. How can Dr Soekarno reconcile Australia's mandate over Papua with these claims, and how long will it be before, either by infiltration or bluff, he takes over the whole of New Guinea?

Now, as never before, we need a strong man at the helm. Someone to say he shall not pass – a Kennedy, a Khrushchev, someone to say "An attack on West New Guinea will be regarded as an attack on us."

We have a mandate over Papua and its people. More, we have a great debt to repay for their tremendous help to our fighting men during that war against Japan. Finally, New Guinea's great resources cannot be lost to us.

Here is Munich all over again – the bullying, the bluster, the lies. "Give us the Sudetenland and we will be satisfied." After that, there were Czechoslovakia and Poland. And now "give us West New Guinea and we'll be happy" – and after that ....?

Letters, A Rigby. I am amazed and dismayed by our Foreign Minister, Sir Garfield Barwick's complacency regarding West New Guinea. Dr Soekarno is a dictator and we who have lived through all the years of this century know from bitter experience that there is no limit to a dictator's ambition.

First a demand and then fulfillment; then another and another. Now what would be this dictator's next demand?

Obviously the rest of the island, then the surrounding smaller islands and later, the major prize, Australia. Have we forgotten Japan? The Eastern Power that holds Australia holds the world.

We Australians are living in a fool's paradise. We think that if we were attacked someone would come to the rescue. Who? We know now that we are defenceless. That should awaken us. A strong leader should sound the alarm and set to work to remake our Armed Forces. Leaders of all parties should tell the people that we must live part of our lives for the future generations. If we fail to do this Australia may become an Asiatic country within 50 years.

Letters, C Meeking, Queenscliff. There is a proper alternative to Australia "taking its stand by the side of the Dutch." If we fight alongside Holland, the military outcome cannot be assessed, although the prospect of what could happen to us from action by some of Indonesia's "supporters" is unpleasant. But certain immediate results can be guessed.

SEATO would be destroyed; our "great allies," who would be unlikely to come to our aid, would be acutely embarrassed; other world tensions would increase to near breaking point; we would incur the lasting enmity of our large neighbor, Indonesia, and the hostility of all other Asian nations, with whom we must live and trade; and there would be serious political effects in Holland and on NATO.

LESS WEIGHTY STUFF

Every time I start a new book, I have to pack a lot of background into the first few pages. That is what I have just done. But after that you deserve a break, so I have pulled together a few Letters to show that the entire world was not as solemn as my first few pages.

Letters, Florence Carter. One continually reads about hikers getting separated from their groups and becoming lost in mountainous areas, thus endangering their lives and causing untold anxiety to their folk and needless expense to the community.

I suggest – call it old-fashioned if you will – that every bushwalker, or hiker, or Boy Scout, should have as part of his equipment an ordinary cowbell, which can be heard at long distances and would be ideal to direct searchers to the person or persons lost.

Letters, H Callan. As suggested by Miss F Carter, the carrying of a cow-bell would certainly help in locating lost hikers, but the extra weight would be a problem and the sound might not travel in hilly country.

More effective and much lighter in weight would be a transistor-operated "radio-howler," small enough to transmit 10-20 miles on a special frequency. Operated for a few minutes each hour, the lost hikers' position could be pinpointed and homed on by a relief party without loss of time. Several sets could be made available on application to centres such as the Katoomba police station.

Operating on the same principle by modern use of the wonderful transistor, the policeman's whistle could now become a wireless policeman's whistle. In a bad "spot" or in urgent need of assistance, all a policeman would have to do would be to press a spot on his tunic and within minutes police cars could be racing to his assistance.

Letters, R Brimble. I fully agree with the two suggestions for bushwalkers who may become lost, but upon enquiring, I have found cowbells and radio howlers extremely hard to purchase.

After much walking experience I have found that a Chinese gong works equally as well and is more readily carried and purchased.

A SILLY MOMENT

Let me digress for a moment. As I write these books, sometimes a really silly Letter is printed, and it starts off a series of responses that are equally silly and really might not have been written at all. But the end result is a series of Letters, spread over a week or two, that are fully capricious and entertaining. Of course, the three Letters above fit into this pattern.

I have just re-read my **1942** book. For Australia, **that year was our darkest ever.** Early on, we realised that more and more of our menfolk would be killed and maimed and captured, and our lives would suddenly be altogether different with the necessary austerity measures introduced. After that, it seemed likely, very likely, that this country would actually be invaded by the Japs. And really there was little we could do about it.

Let me return now to the series-of-silly-Letters talk. In all of the year **1942,** using the *Sydney Morning Herald* as the yardstick, there were **only two** such series published, and these were in October and December, after it became clear that the War had missed our shores.

By contrast, in **1962**, using the *SMH* again, in the **first month alone** there were **five** such series. I happen to know that this was not a fluke, and that the same rate was preserved for the rest of the year. **This, I am happy to tell you, speaks to the mood of the nation at this time.** There was a bit of a recession at the moment, but people were not daunted. They were ready to be capricious, frivolous, carefree, as they chose, and at the same time, pursue their serious objectives like jobs and houses and motor cars. While keeping an eye on the multitude of kids that they had given birth to, they were starting to become a nation of go-getters, of people largely free from overseas baggage, of people who just wanted to do **what they wanted to do**. And, looking ahead, nobody saw any reason why they could not do this. This was the mood at the start of **1962.**

TRIVIA

Letters, B Watson. Driving home from Bilgola Beach in the late afternoon one day last week, I was amazed at the large number of hitch-hikers along the way. Without exaggeration, there were at least 20 to 25 young boys and girls in Newport shopping centre alone "raising their thumbs."

Participants in this mode of travelling seem to be in the main teenagers and it would appear that they are not being discouraged by their parents. Unfortunately, too, the motoring public are tolerating them and it is all the more alarming when one sees these hitch-hikers thumbing for rides along bus routes and within very short distances of railway stations.

Letters, R Maxwell. I would like to point out to B H Watson why teenagers are likely to "raise their thumbs" along beach roads.

For a great number of beach-lovers, it is a question of using public transport at least three times between home and the beach, making the trip a three or four hour journey, and an expensive one for many teenagers. The same applies on the trip back. If on the other hand they hitch-hike, it is possible to reach the beaches in less than half the time, and hours of sunshine are saved, as well as money. In any case, how many beaches are served by railways?

Let us hope that the Australian spirit of mateship has not decayed to the extent to which Mr Watson's attitude appears to indicate.

A FEW INFORMATIVE LETTERS

Letters, A McNish, Association of Blind Citizens, Sydney. After reading of the early completion of a "fragrance garden" for the blind in Phillip Park, the Association of Blind Citizens feels compelled to record its criticism of this project.

This garden will consist of raised flower beds filled with specially selected perfumed blooms, the beds will also be furnished with Braille plaques bearing the names of the flowers growing there. And as an added attraction there will be the sound of tinkling fountains.

On first appearances this may seem to be a thoroughly charming idea, but on closer examination one will recognise in the project a mere display of sentimental thinking which contributes nothing to the welfare of the blind. We are not alone in this view, the Blinded Veterans' Association of America, and the American Foundation for the Blind, probably the largest organisations working for the blind in America, have expressed their disapproval of "fragrance gardens."

It is generally conceded that by their nature fragrance gardens create an unfavourable image of blind people in the minds of the public. If the garden is completed we find it difficult to believe that any blind person would go to the trouble of struggling through the city for the pleasure of going on exhibition in the garden. Let us have gardens by all means, but not "fragrance gardens."

Letters, J Somerville. It was indeed refreshing to read in your columns of the successful use of the breathalyser in securing the convictions and punishment of intoxicated car drivers, and the Victorian government is to be complimented on having the moral courage to use this instrument in dealing with the kind of people who are causing the appalling slaughter on our highways. A few more sentences like those imposed in Victoria last week will quickly reduce the number of roadhogs and make travelling safer in that State. Traffic laws in NSW make it very difficult for police to secure convictions for "driving under the influence."

The great value of the breathalyser is in the fact that it is completely impartial, and reveals with scientific exactness the percentage of alcohol in the blood of the accused. This, considered in conjunction with the other evidence submitted, enables a judge and jury to form a sound judgment.

Breathalyser testing would greatly reduce over-indulgence in hotels and other places, thus removing a principal cause of road accidents, injuries and deaths. The popular "one for the road" often means two for the undertaker, and more for the hospitals. The breathalyser would certainly ensure many more beds being available for long-waiting patients in city hospitals.

Letters, J Swift. How long is the community to tolerate the offensive custom of scattering the cremated remains of individuals around the landscape at the behest of the departed or of relatives? No place is sacred: public gardens, inland waters and ocean beaches are favourite targets.

One could match this form of exhibitionism by ordaining that one's articulated skeleton be suspended in the front garden on a favourite jacaranda tree.

Letters, Peter Brooks. As the body is the shell left by man's spirit, why all the fuss about where it is placed? People would rather look at tradition and not at the facts. Cremation and sea burials give the chance for the body to take its natural passage back to God's earth. I think the marble slab is outdated.

Surely it would be better to plant a tree, and as it grows sprinkle the ashes of the deceased around its base, so the tree may be nourished by them. This way one could have a beautiful growing memorial to a loved one.

Letters, R Anderson. A recent road accident in Victoria has prompted me to write this letter in the hope that some publicity can be given to perhaps the least publicised aspect of road safety – overcrowded and overloaded (overweighted) vehicles.

Most drivers are aware of the dangers and the majority make a sincere effort to avoid overloading. But then some of these same drivers would think nothing of bundling six or seven children into a car for a run to the beach. Just because two or three kids equal the weight of one adult, they assume the vehicle is not overloaded. Perhaps so. The driver has avoided overloading but in doing so has overcrowded his car.

Apart from driver distraction, the symptoms of overcrowding are not quite so obvious as those of overloading, but in an accident the result can be disastrous. The primary cause could be a second party, a drunken driver or an oncoming car on the wrong side of the road. To prevent this type of accident, where often a whole family is involved and often with sad results, motorists should not exceed the car manufacturer's maximum seating capacities, even if the vehicle is still within the maximum weight limit.

SOME TRIVIA

Astro, a golden Labrador from Tamworth, has been **trained for ten months to become a tracker for the local Civil Defence airborne rescue team**. On his first birthday this week, he was ready to take his first jump from a plane, all trussed up in a parachute. His trainer ordered "Jump, Astro" and the dog leapt from the plane. But his parachute failed to open, and he plunged 650 feet to his death.

Author Barbara Cartland: "I always preserve the virginity of my heroine for 360 pages."

FEBRUARY NEWS ITEMS

The NSW Department of Education has **introduced co-education in all of its larger schools for the entire six years of primary school.** Previously, children had been segregated in the final three years.

The **Queen's locked liquor cabinet** has been raided and **several bottles of top whisky and gin have been taken**. Police suspect that workmen installing a central heating system in Windsor Castle are responsible.

Dr Justin Andrews, of the US National Institute of Allergy and Infective Disease, said that **American scientists would have a cure for the common cold within five years,** and it would completely disappear within ten.

Betsy, an elephant with Sole Brothers' Circus in South Australia, **trampled a male journalist to death** a few days ago. It is now suggested that Betsy should be destroyed. No firm decision has been made of the matter as yet.

From Robert Menzies. "As the proposals were entirely agreeable to me, I thought they were all very intelligent."

A Twist dancer, seeking compensation. "I moved in the wrong direction at the wrong time."

John Ellison, Librarian. **Fourteen** of Sydney's 35 metropolitan municipalities have **yet to start their library services**.

Unemployment in January hit post-War record low.
American astronaut, John Glenn, circled the globe three times. He was America's first man to do so, following on from two Russians in the previous year.

The US and Fidel Castro of Cuba started to flay each other. The US imposed duty on some of Cuba's exports and gave that nation several mouthfuls of abuse and advice. Castro in return breathed defiance and showed no sign of being intimidated. Watch this space.

Overflow from septic tanks was flowing into the streets in several of Sydney's poshest new suburbs, such as St Ives. Various writers and authorities blamed this for the increased incidence of polio. The laying of sewer pipes was proceeding at a snail's pace, said several writers, and one estimated that, at the current rate, it would take 200 years to cover all of existing Sydney.

Nerida Blair, the daughter of well-known aboriginal singer, Harold Blair, today had her first day at an exclusive Melbourne school, Tintern Girls' Grammar School. The principal said there had been no question about accepting Nerida, and she was quite sure that no parents would object either....

Mr Blair said "This is the fulfillment of one of my greatest ambitions. I want every aboriginal in Australia to fight for education for themselves and their children. One day, **I dream that an aboriginal will be Prime Minister of Australia.**"

Mr Nott, of Sydney, wrote complaining that the **Government had placed a ban on the export of budgerigars.** Not only that, he noted, the ban has been extended to fertile eggs. He pointed out that millions of dozens of hen eggs are exported, and they are simply eaten. Fertile budgie eggs exported would bring this nation's name into millions of homes overseas, and bring us the goodwill that a superior product generates.

Australians Joan Sutherland and Robin Lovejoy were acclaimed last night overseas. Sutherland for her triumphant debut in Rome. Loveday for his new production of Puccini's La Boheme for the Saddler's Wells Opera Company.

"Nudity doesn't mix with motherhood." Jayne Mansfield.

From the Duchess of Bedford: " Everything is crested at the Abbey. The Duke would not sleep in pyjamas unless they are crested.

Rev Alan Walker thinks that "There is a real danger that the **absurd Easter bunny** will become the symbol of Easter."

Australia's first Memorial Park will be built on the outskirts of Sydney. It will be modeled on America's Forest Lawn Cemetery, and will have 172 acres of lawn, with bronze plaques replacing headstones. Plots would cost One Hundred Pounds, a saving of Fifty Pounds on conventional graves with kerbing and headstones. A special "Wall of Remembrance" would be built for people who wished to be cremated.

NATIONAL NEWS

The Federal Government reacted at last to signals that suggested the economy was doing it fairly tough. It introduced a number of measures that cut duties on imported goods and allowed a number of products to enter this nation that had been forbidden just over a year ago. For example, the tariff on British cars was cut from a huge 30 per cent down to 22 per cent. The Leader of the Opposition was far from impressed, and said the measures were too little, too late, and that this was a typical stop-go policy. As usual, such platitudes got little attention.

West Irian went pretty quiet for the month. At one stage, the US got the Dutch riled by refusing landing rights (in Japan) to Dutch planes that were carrying troops to New Guinea. No one could figure out why they did this, and the best suggestion was that they were saying that the US was not one hundred per cent behind the Dutch. No one quite knew why the Americans did not just say this to the Dutch, but in any case, the matter passed over in a week or so.

Meanwhile, Soekarno was building up his forces near the coast of West Irian, and generally rattling his sword. The Australian Government was saying it wanted peace, and was being accused here and there of being pacifist, and that surely all of this was just a re-enactment of the appeasement of Hitler.

Letters, W Mason. Are we selling out cheaply in West New Guinea? Is the Menzies government prepared to surrender without even firing a verbal shot? Are our "powerful friends and allies" too absorbed, in bolstering up a crumbling position in South-East Asia, to see that the Communists are likely to bypass South-East Asia altogether in their infiltration southwards?

The future of West New Guinea is vital to Australia and our present laissez-faire attitude is deplorable. We could well combat any Indonesian claim by **a counter-claim** for extension of our trusteeship of East New Guinea to cover the whole of New Guinea in collaboration with the Dutch. Such joint control, perhaps under supervision by the United Nations, would be in the best interests of self-determination of the native peoples of the whole territory.

We should entirely discount any assurances by present Indonesian rulers that they will have no future hankerings for East New Guinea, especially in view of their boast that they have the solid backing of the Soviet Union.

Our present attitude is that of an ostrich with its head buried in the sand, while the Indonesian rulers are gleefully pulling feathers out of its tail.

Letters, Roland Hill. I am in entire agreement with the editorial "Appeasement, but Call It Something Else!" One would have thought that Australia would be more concerned with justice and honour, instead of cowering in fear of our Asian neighbours. If America and Britain refuse to support Holland against blatant aggression, one should despise their selfish outlook, not use it as an excuse to follow suit.

Over the past few months, the various announcements of our Government's views on the West New Guinea problem have made me feel sick in the stomach – a most unpleasant feeling, especially after spending six years fighting for freedom for ourselves. Mr Menzies appears to lack something that Mr Churchill has in abundance.

I have been a Liberal Party supporter all my life, but now it appears to be changed to the Menzies Party, and, while that state of affairs lasts, I and my wife will never support it.

Letters, W Willmore.   Grateful thanks to the "Herald" for pointing out to us that Mr Menzies is the right man in the right place.

By daily publishing Mr Calwell's biased and persistent niggling, you have shown his smallness and his inability to accept the fact that "teacher didn't make him class prefect." You show clearly that he is unfit for leadership.

Comment. Most Australians at this stage could remember back twenty years to 1942, and knew what a real War was. The threat that Indonesia posed was quite dinky compared to that, so regardless of the rights or wrongs of the situation, most Australians were not terribly concerned at this stage.

ETHICS OF DOCTORS

A few weeks ago, a collision between two cars occurred in an inner Sydney suburb, and the occupants urgently needed medical treatment. The situation at the time, however, was that Australian cities did not provide 24-hour emergency services as we know them today, but rather doctors were called from their homes to the scene of the accident. In this case, no doctors who were willing to come out could be found, and a person died, who might or might not, have been saved.

In a knee-jerk response to this, the State Government started talking about some **sort of compulsion** being imposed on doctors to force them to respond to emergency calls at night.

Letters, Medico. With the threat of penalties or even deregistration of doctors who fail to answer "emergency calls" it is hoped that the Australian Medical Association will take positive steps to protect its members.

For many years attendance at street accidents has been regarded as a voluntary service with no question of recompense. Having helped the ambulancemen load the casualties, one can hardly then ask their names and addresses with a view to sending an account. Besides which, an account if sent would not receive attention until the Third Party action was settled some years later. It is not uncommon to find two or three of one's colleagues at a street accident as well as the ambulance, all of whom have been rung anonymously by well-meaning members of the public.

What would happen to a doctor when so sent for if he was doing an equally important job elsewhere or his car was being serviced while he was in his surgery? Will a doctor have to keep a certified diary of his whereabouts in case he is reported for not attending an emergency? The worried relative who calls the doctor "in an emergency" is seldom the best judge of its seriousness.

Thus one morning at 2 o'clock I received a brief message: "Come at once. It's urgent." On my arrival I found a worried householder, unable to get police assistance hearing a would-be burglar at the window, had sent for the doctor. Fortunately the intruder had gone before my arrival.

On another morning at 4 o'clock in pouring rain, lightning struck the chimney pot. No one was hurt but the good folk sent for doctor in view of the "emergency."

On a third occasion late at night a call to a case of "acute appendicitis" turned out be a scheme to get members home from a drunken party by ambulance because they were out of petrol.

If the Minister wishes to introduce and police an "Emergency Call" service it could be done by using the resident medical officers from public hospitals and the ambulance service as is done in America. A special phone number could be allotted or the police emergency numbers used. Private doctors by and large have done a good job in the past and accepted conscription without demur. Socialistic controls now will not give the public a better service.

Letters, Doctor, Parramatta. I have attended patients when I have been running a fever and felt dreadful, when, in fact, I have been more ill than the patient. Should a doctor be legally forced to work under these circumstances?

Where is the line to be drawn between a just refusal and "infamous conduct"? Should a doctor be forced, usually on a Sunday evening, to attend a man with his head cut in a drunken brawl, a person with a cold of five days' duration now running a fever, a person with a small cut for a tetanus injection (skin tests and proper precautions may last one hour), or a man with a boil of several days' duration?

I find it is impossible to assess for certain a patient's condition over the telephone or via a messenger. In reality, therefore, the Act will force doctors to attend all comers. I do not think that is reasonable.

Letters, Cynical But Dedicated Medico. In the first place, the principle of compulsion is utterly wrong in a free democracy and still more so if restricted to one small group in the community. If we are going to be ruled by a dictatorship (which God forbid), let everyone be included – plumbers (to attend to burst water pipes on the spot), electricians (to repair the fridge on the blink), TV technicians (to attend promptly to avert a riot among the children). We could go on indefinitely! Why single out the poor, weary, overworked GPs?

In the second place, compulsion of any sort seriously impairs the doctor-patient relationship, as has happened in England since the national health scheme came into being.

But I guarantee that the medical profession as a whole have far higher principles and are more conscious of their duty to the community than most politicians.

Thirdly, it will require a committee with the wisdom of Solomon to define and qualify an "emergency call." Like "Medico", I, in common with most GPs, have been pulled out of bed at all hours of the night and early morning often for completely frivolous and unnecessary reasons.

Many rush calls have been from people sick for days and others hardly sick at all. However, if there is any doubt about the "emergency," the great majority of GPs will attend willingly. But it is little wonder that some doctors are a little testy on the phone at 2 o'clock in the morning, after they have probably just completed a 15-hour day and usually a 70 to 80 hour week.

I think Mr Sheahan and his team would be better employed in providing more and better hospital accommodation than wasting time on this completely unnecessary and insulting legislation.

Letters, Fifteen Years A City Practitioner. While the right hand of the Government is busy along these lines, the left hand of the government is driving medical men off the roads and out of the city. It may be said this is exaggeration. However, there is no place at which a doctor may leave his car without risk of having it towed away or being "booked" and without being eventually required to appear in court – and this merely for continuing a long-established service to the public.

At the moment, I have about six summonses to appear in court – my explanations of the circumstances of the use of my car in and around the city not having been the wish of the Government that alacrity in "doing calls" be more than encouraged, then it is essential that this desirable humane service to the individual be facilitated rather than rendered impossible by some busy section of the administration which may have lost sight of the overall picture briefly.

It is in the interests of the individual, whoever he is, that his medical attendant be enabled to reach him in his urgent need with as few man-made difficulties as possible.

Letters, B O'Sullivan. The few doctors that the legislation is aimed at will become even more inaccessible. The rest of the profession will carry on as usual, except for the threat that hangs over their heads, until the effort of coping with non-urgent "emergency" calls proves too much. Then they, too, will ignore the incessant ring of the telephone and the real emergency case will be left without medical attention.

Who will get the blame then? The nearest local practitioner, the specialist who only sees the patient during office hours, or the hospital out-patients' department, which has no call service? Undoubtedly the local practitioner will be the scapegoat and will have to submit to the anxiety and loss of time resulting from the inevitable inquiry.

No sane doctor condones a state where patients cannot get urgent medical attention when needed, but mere legislation will not provide it. The remedy lies with the medical profession itself and every doctor has a responsibility to provide an emergency service for his patients at all hours. This can be done by organisation into rotas, partnerships or group practices. Herein lies the answer, not in more bureaucratic legislation.

Comment. The Government came under widespread criticism for its proposed legislation. So much so that, by the end of the month, it was making noises about whether some other solution, to this real problem, was possible.

BIRTH CONTROL BY PILLS

Human contraception methods were suddenly in the news. Up till now, there were some wonderful methods of preventing conception that had been practiced for years and years. One of these, abstinence, was not highly thought of. Another, taught by religious institutions, in particular the Catholic Church, was a conspicuous failure in practice, as witnessed by the large families that sprang up wherever it was practised. There were all sorts of nostrums that were even less successful.

But now there was **The Pill.** This was based on science, and had the support of many doctors, was backed by a limited amount of overseas experience, and had the wholesale support, not surprisingly, of the world's pharmaceutical companies. Users of it were told not to use it for too long, perhaps two months on and one month off. They were told not to use it jointly with other medications, and that it might even out their temperament. They were told by many people that it was a mortal sin to use it at all. They were told all sorts of confusing and contradictory claims, but many women were not daunted. They saw that it offered a new freedom for their lives, and started popping with or without relish. **Meanwhile, the pros and cons battle raged.** This first Letter stirred up a real hornet's nest.

Letters, (Dr.) E D'Abrera, Lewisham Hospital. It is bad enough for bodies like the British Family

Planning Association to add the contraceptive pill to their armaments for destroying the human race, but it is worse for the "Herald" to "educate" its reading public with "strip-tease" cartoons on the contraceptive pill, especially when the "pill" is coated with such a generous helping of half-truths. Is it a "safe and easy means of population control" as the "Population Explosion" strips make out?

In a leading article, the "British Medical Journal" (September 16, 1961) expressed concern on the possible unknown future biological effects which suppression of ovulation over a long period would have on the mothers of today and the grandmothers (if any) of tomorrow.

Reputable gynaecologists, pathologists and endocrinologists view with alarm the prospect of large numbers of nauseated, hirsute women hemorrhaging irregularly from highly abnormal uterine tissues and they wonder whether it would be wise to expose newly married women and young mothers (for these are the groups that would lap up the "Herald's" cartoons) to gynaecologial and endocrine risks that no one can now foresee.

These pills have a virilisng effect on female fetuses in utero and one just shudders to think of the possible outcome were such pills to be inadvertently taken by pregnant women at a time when their pregnancy was yet indeterminate. These pills are now being sold "over the counter" and "under the counter" in chemists' shops – soon they will be available in "milk bars" and "barbers' saloons."

Perhaps in the end the contraceptive pill may achieve more than the atom bomb and atomic fallout.

Letters, Pill-Taker. I am one of the group of "young mothers". The groups that would lap up the "Herald's' cartoons," referred to by Dr E D'Abrera, though I have been taking the birth-control pills for three months now, i.e., before your cartoon appeared.

Before changing my previous contraceptive for the new pills, I inquired from three general practitioners about their safety, to find that each of their wives was taking them; I then consulted my own gynaecologist, and he assured me that they were perfectly safe for my health, health of any future children I might decide to have, and for my present desire not to have any children.

Naturally, therefore, I read with concern Dr D'Abrera's letter, as I don't want my future unborn children to be abnormal; in fairness to the pills, I must say that I have had no nausea; my hair (in the wrong places) has not increased, and no haemorrhage; a month ago my uterine tissues were normal. I am concerned, therefore, with the possibility that all these things may yet happen to me; and even more concerned that so many doctors are dispensing such dangerous advice with perfect calm and so much confidence that they are exposing their own wives and future children to all these dangers.

Letters, Ernest Cameron. The final paragraph of the letter by "Another Femme" clearly indicates that her thinking is wrong.

The Catholic Church has not a double standard – it condemns pre-marital intercourse under all circumstances for both sexes.

These pills – and I express no opinion on their use – are to be prescribed by a medical practitioner. Heaven help us if they become generally available over the counter for promiscuous use by the un-marrieds!

Letters, Mother. I had thought to bring up my sweet 15-year-old daughter in certain apparently outmoded virtues, in the belief that she would ultimately find happiness with a husband with like standards.

Shall I now change my doctor, who is a Roman Catholic and doubtless opposed to the use of contraceptive pills, entice a supply from another doctor and present them to my daughter with instructions to join the human barnyard depicted by some of your correspondents – at the risk of her health, since no gynaecologist could convince me that nature is going to submit without retribution to being turned on and off at will?

Comment. There will be more comment on the Pill as the year passes, and more and more women consider using it.

GOD'S WILL FOR TRADE UNIONS

Three factory owners argued in the Arbitration Court today that their factories should be exempt from Trade Union Provisions, such as Union inspection, because Union awards were against the will of God. "Unionism is contrary to what God has in mind for man, and forces man onto an entirely different path from His." The factory owners were all sincere men, of good character. They would not say what form of religion they practised, though the word "Brethren" was often used. Their exemption was refused.

COMPLETE TRIVIA

Letters, (Mrs) W Kelly. I wish to say a good word for **non-iron cottons**. I have three frocks which are made from British cottons, and my sons have several shirts each. These have all been in use for about three years, and have never known the touch of an iron. But they all bear well-known labels and brand names which carry a guarantee.

Letters, C Whitmont. Let me say, as a shirt manufacturer, that my company has never branded a shirt as "non-iron," for we believe there is no such thing as a 100 per cent no-iron cotton shirt. They all need at least touching up with an iron.

Mr Wills' remarks about heat bonding of collar linings may be correct in some cases, but manufacturers who have real know-how do use this method successfully, for, done properly, it makes a far better collar than those made by other methods.

WISDOM FROM A LEGEND

Charlie Chaplin: "you don't really think until you are seventy."

MARCH NEWS ITEMS

The Queen will arrive in Sydney on March 4. It will be proclaimed a **public holiday for NSW.**

The Government proposes to provide a welcome by 75,000 schoolchildren **at the Sydney Showground. The NSW Teachers' Federation opposes this.** It will involve much expense for some children, and some children will be "herded" there against their will.

Newcastle was the first location outside the major cities to transmit television. A commercial station was opened yesterday, and a National station (ABC) would open soon.

Letter from Pupils in 5A and 6A, Coogee Public School. "We are quite sad to think that our children may never be able to see koalas and other rare Australian animals, which are dying out for want of suitable sanctuaries and proper scientific care. **The loss of the lovely, cuddly, adorable koala** will be a bad blot on Australia's history, and we want to prevent this threatened tragedy."

The first "heart pace-makers" were evolving rapidly. A Mr Miller yesterday had an operation in which contact wires were inserted into his heart. The other end of the wires were attached to a device that he carried in his pocket. The external device weighs about a pound (450 grams).

The newly-elected Federal Government, led by Menzies, survived a censure motion by a single vote, emphasising how precarious his tenure is.

The Director of the International Commission for the Prevention of Alcoholism, a visiting American, said that there were a large number of hidden women alcoholics in Australia. The fact that they were hidden resulted from the stigma placed on women entering bars here.

Cubans are facing strict rationing of food, soap, toothpaste, detergents and other goods. This is because of a "brutal economic blockade", according to Prime Minister Castro. The "Yankee Imperialists" were making desperate efforts to destroy the Cuban Revolution.

The system of on-the-spot fines will start in NSW from next Sunday. If a person admits guilt, he can pay by mail or at a police station. If not, he will be summonsed after 21 days.

Dr Raggett, of the Department of National Development, said that cheap nuclear explosions could be used to build dams and harbours round Australia. Vacant land outside Adelaide could capture the surplus waters of the Murray.

In the north of Australia, one big bang could be used to create a harbour that could be used by 30,000-ton ships. Radio-activity in waters would not be a problem in five years because of research being conducted.

Danish comedian and pianist, Victor Borge, is now performing at Sydney's Her Majesty's Theatre. You should see him if you can make it.

MOTHERHOOD

The introduction of the Pill was seen, by many women, as giving more freedom to do what they wanted with their own bodies. But many women, often different from the Pill-swallowers, were more concerned with the roles of mothers in society. Many thought that the traditional role of the stay-at-home mother was necessary for the welfare of the family. Many of these were also **happy to be the clucky hen** looking after her brood, and it was sheer joy to do that job. Others saw the role of the mother as absolute boredom, hated the housework that went with the job, and wanted nothing more than to resign.

In mid-March, interest in this topic, and in contraception, flared for a few weeks.

Letters, Mother of Five. Most contraceptives don't work well enough and it's a perfectly miserable life doing nothing but cleaning and washing, cooking, ironing, forcing the kids to do their homework and listening to my husband complain about no money and no chance of a holiday.

Sometimes when I start a book or go to a decent play, or read some of those CAB things husband brings home, I realise how much there is in life that I'm missing. I just feel like a machine and what's the good of living to 70 or 80 if you feel like this all the time?

Now, with the youngest at kindergarten, I'll be able to get out of the house for a while and see that there really is a world outside. And I'll have time to read books all the way through without being interrupted or shouted at.

Letters, Analyst. "Mother of Five" in her difficulties and her yearning for the "better things of life" overlooks the fact that the prime object of marriage is the production of children.

She states that contraceptives did not work well enough so she was saddled with five children. Surely it is not being a machine to carry out the world's highest vocation, namely, the rearing of children. If our way of life makes this rearing difficult, the fault lies in our way of life, not in nature's fecundity.

Letters, (Mrs) M Nelson. One of the women who rushed into print in defence of their contraceptive pill-taking wrote that her gynaecologist had assured her that there would be no side effects. If this is so, has the gynaecologist read the leading article in the issue of the "British Medical Journal" referred to by Dr D'Abrera?

If he has not, then why not? If he has, is he in possession of more reliable information and what is it? Could it be that these women are unwitting guinea-pigs in what is, as yet, an inconclusive experiment?

The danger of unauthorised dissemination of these pills is another point raised by Dr D'Abrera. If the risks of prescribing them are to be run, is it too much to ask that production and distribution should be rigidly controlled in some such fashion as in the handling of the Salk vaccine? Given the present-day attitude to birth-control, is there any drug likely to be in greater demand?

"Chemist" discounts the possibility of birth-control pills being sold "over the counter" and "under the counter" but at least admits the possibility of unlawful demand. When demand is strong enough (and profits attractive) surely a black-market will spring up to meet it.

In one way, Dr D'Abrera's letter seems to me to be unanswerable. Yet, I am astonished there has not been even one doctor's reply either in refutation or support. Is it unethical for members of the medical profession to give some indication in the columns of the "Herald" of their attitudes to prescribing and regulating the use of this latest panacea for infelicitous fertility?

Letters, (Mrs) Nanette Bourke. That "Analyst's" arguments are, of course, not directed against the new "pills" but against contraceptives in general is no reason why they should go unanswered.

Nothing annoys me more than sanctimonious talk about the "noble vocation of motherhood." If society really felt this way, perhaps it would treat mothers with more consideration, providing ramps instead of steps at railway stations, storage for prams and strollers on buses and trains, delivery of all purchases, and so on. However, most people, from landlords to other shoppers, regard mothers with young children as the worst nuisance there is.

Recently I had the temerity to visit the Duke of Bedford's exhibition, accompanied by my children, aged 5 and 1, and if I'd walked in with a couple of mangy dogs I couldn't have been eyed more disapprovingly than I was by most of those present.

They were more impressed by the Duke's nobility than mine.

However, let us assume for a moment that motherhood is a noble vocation, does it necessarily follow that all women should be expected to become mothers? Most of us consider medicine a noble vocation, but no one would suggest that all men become doctors. What sort of a society is it that decides the occupations of its members, noble or otherwise? Most women are not opposed to motherhood, but they do object to having no choice.

There are a few exceptional ones who love children so much that they want a large family, and whose gifts are such that they are able to give each child the love and attention it needs. Most of us, however, prefer two or three children, a number we feel we can care for and educate properly, without reducing ourselves to mindless drudges is the process.

Those who think that mothers should be willing to forgo books, drama and music underestimate the demands of motherhood. It is not enough to clothe and feed a child, he must be educated, morally and mentally, and no mother whose mind is dulled by drudgery can rear an intellectually active and eager child.

I see little merit in bringing increasing numbers of children into the world so that they may die of starvation or as the victims of a thermo-nuclear war. What we need are not more bodies but more minds capable of solving the problems of our already overcrowded world.

Letters, Social Worker. "Another Femme" seems to be taking a very unrealistic view if she imagines that "the new contraceptive pills are to mean an end to the tragedy of the unmarried mother and the illegitimate child."

The question of the unmarried mother generally lies far deeper than effective means of contraception. The unmarried mother comes from all classes of society and all ranges of intelligence, and with the possible exception of the really dull girl, the pregnancy is often a symptom of a deeper psychological problem such as emotional insecurity, hatred of a parent, etc. She may have the intelligence to use contraceptives, but because it is her present emotional problem that has got her into the situation, she is not conscious of the future and therefore does not think in terms of contraception.

The Church leaders have every right to express "horror and alarm" at "the number of teenage girls pregnant and suffering from venereal disease." Surely thinking people would be disturbed about this in terms of human tragedy, but I don't think this can be taken as moral condemnation of the girls concerned. Most Churches are concerned in prevention and treatment. Leading Churches offer hostel or hospital care and an endeavour to rehabilitate these girls through methods based on modern social work practice in which moral condemnation has no place.

The fact that the men don't warrant a mention is surely biological and cannot be taken as condoning their behaviour. It is the girl who needs medical aid, emotional and financial and possibly accommodation help, but it is wrong to assume that the man evades all responsibility. Maintenance proceedings can be taken, and how many boys and girls have been forced into an unwanted marriage by parental or social pressure.

Letters, Contented Drudge. Nanette Bourke's suggestion that women rearing more than two or three children must be willing to forgo "books, drama and music" to become "mindless drudges" would be insulting if it were not more than a little pathetic.

Her further suggestion that children of large families tend to grow up with their dear little intellects stunted through lack of attention is quite hilarious. Nothing sharpens a child's sensitivity and intellectual curiosity more than interaction and competition with other children.

Of course child bearing and rearing is in many respects a drudging affair, particularly in these difficult days, but no more so than many of the so-called "careers" hankered after by women who would find even one child an intolerable burden. But it at least possesses the compensations of being challenging, endlessly fascinating, and of providing great and lasting satisfaction.

The all-too-current I-want-to-give-my-children-everything-I-didn't-have attitude is, more often than not, a purely selfish one which is the root cause of the delinquency emanating currently from better-class homes. Children require food, shelter, affection, discipline and guidance from their parents. If the luxuries can be added to these necessities, well and good, but they can survive and prosper very well without them.

I myself have five children ranging in age from 2 to 8. There are many occasions when I could ignobly but cheerfully knock their heads together, but I can assure Mrs Bourke that I have never at any time felt that I was an uncultured and mindless drudge.

Comment. What a mixed bag. There were about thirty such Letters published, and the high diversity was maintained throughout. All I can deduce is that this part of the world was in great flux.

PUBLIC DISPLAYS OF THE INDECENT?

Public decency was a matter much discussed. A few months ago, the wearing of bikini swimsuits had attracted attention, but now three other matters got onto the agenda.

The first of these was men's swimsuits, made of the new nylon material, that in some cases was quite revealing of things that, some thought, should have remained hidden.

Letters, Styles Parkes. While I have seen briefer men's swimsuits on the Continent, they are less offensive than those in Australia because of the thin nature of the material used in the manufacture here.

A very popular type of trunks, made of nylon and/or terylene, is by far the most revealing, especially when wet, and should be made with a thicker inner garment.

I recently met my teenage sons and their mates at the beach wearing these trunks at a dangerously low level and in a blasé manner.   When I reprimanded them, they admitted that they were aware that at least one beach and one swimming pool had banned these swimsuits; however, it was considered "sharp" to wear them and get away with as much – or should I say less? – as possible.

The unfortunate thing is that the culprits are mostly teenagers and surf club members who are quite aware of, and encourage, this form of vulgar exhibition.

Letters, D J R.   D Dunn asserts that brief swimsuits (of a kind accepted abroad for the last 30 years) "offend the majority."

Prurient old women of both sexes have always been with us, but that they comprise "the majority" I refuse to believe.

Letters, J Moore.   I would like to suggest to your correspondent Styles Parkes that he devote less time to observing the "vulgar exhibition" by "teenagers and surf club members," and more time to encouraging them in the pursuit of the surf club and swimming activities.   After reading his letter, one sees a picture of the public having to cover their eyes from the "vulgar" display as the surf club boys carry in someone they have rescued.

As an active member of a swimming club, I consider the terylene trunks, so popular today, to be the most functional type of men's swimsuit at present on the market.   Anyone associated with competitive swimming is aware of the increase in speed gained by wearing them.   They are light and easy to carry, which is particularly useful for those of us who swim either before or after work, or during the lunch hour. They dry quickly, which is an advantage not only for carrying, but also because it helps to prevent the spread of tinea which sometimes occurs with a frequent swimmer. I feel that the widespread use of the terylene trunks is, in fact, due to these advantages in most cases rather than an attempt to be "sharp" or purposely to offend others.

The second of these was concerned with an increasing number of women who were happy enough to reveal more of their bodies than had previously been the custom.

Letters, G A Mulholland. Perhaps the desexing of rapists would be an excellent idea, but would Mrs M Carp also agree to having females desexed for provoking men, parading the streets half dressed, and lying on the beaches even less dressed?

Letters, (Miss) Susan Metcalf. Does Mr Mulholland realise that fashion alone dictates a woman's dress, or undress, not animal cunning? Indeed it's a sad state of affairs in this country, of hopelessly inadequate and insensitive males, that women must revert to comparative nudity to arouse the least masculine response.

Letter, Pat Posetti. I like to see women break with tradition and show more of themselves. But only if they have got something to show. Most Australian women think they can be alluring just by flaunting little bits of their bodies, and gullible males will flock to them. Of course they are right, but who wants a herd of 19-year old dimwits courting them.

The third of these refer to the Shows that were held in every city round the nation each year. The Shows were based on local agriculture, and with the merry-go-round, and dodgem cars and boxing tents, were a number of side-shows, that were often a bit seedy. Two ladies were moved to print.

Letters, Thelma Bate, Country Women's Association. The first part of the show consisted of girls with almost negligible covering, who came in one at a time and progressed around the circle, waggling parts of their anatomy in a shockingly suggestive manner. This was accompanied by a running commentary from a showman with a microphone, a commentary filled with words like "excitement" and "getting stirred up."

In the next part, a girl stood behind glass, and two boys at a time were given rubber suction darts, which they threw at the glass, in the hope that a dart would stick to a spot behind which was a part of girl's body from which they wanted the covering (such as it was) removed. The most successful won the privilege of washing the back of the unclothed girl when she got into her bath.

I left when I could stand no more, glad that none of the boys' mothers were there to see what was being done to their young sons. The other shows were much of a type, that is, strip-tease in one form or other.

Letters, Teenagers' Mother. Recently, in company with my teenage children, I visited Penrith show and was appalled at the "patter" of a commentator outside a tent as he invited young lads to take part in the "preview" of the entertainment they were promised inside.

Thankfully, my sons were just as disgusted and declared in favour of the ring events, but as I stood watching the rush of young lads to partake of the "excitement" and "getting stirred up," I found it very easy to understand why we have the appalling number of young boys involved in rape cases.

THE ARMING OF POLICE

In 1962, many of the police on duty carried revolvers. This was always a matter of minor concern, and in particular they were contrasted with London Bobbies, who were not generally armed. The matter now came to public attention because a Labrador dog in Sydney recently escaped from her back yard, and went to a school yard and boisterously frolicked among the children. A young constable, called to the scene, could not subdue the dog, and shot and killed it. This brought forth some protests, but then the issue was broadened to the more general question of whether our local police should be carrying guns at all in their normal duties.

Letters, F Bland. Have we become so indifferent to our citizen's privileges that we can read without resentment the story of the wanton shooting of a pet pedigree Labrador that had unwittingly strayed from its yard to follow a little girl to school?

This exercise of police power is possibly a legacy of the war years when we placed our liberties in pawn to be exercised as authority thought best for the purpose of winning the war.

Again, the multiplication of Government activities renders it literally impossible for authoritarian abuses to be checked. The arrogant attitude of the transport workers, and of the tug crews, merits treatment meted out to traitors to the State.

These are merely illustrations of the exercise of arbitrary power that is the mark of the slave State. Surely it is time to consider whether we are still to be pushed about like slaves. I suggest the hoisting again of the flag of liberty which too long has been trampled under desecrating feet.

Letters, A Weeks. What effect is this cruel and stupid shooting of the Labrador Bambi, near a big school, going to have on the minds of the pupils of the school? We citizens are trying to teach children that the police are our friends and helpers. Children are very impressionable, and this sad memory will haunt some of them for years to come.

Letters, Casualty Sister. F A Bland writes about "citizens' privileges" and "arrogant attitudes" in regard to the shooting of the Labrador dog Bambi.

Does it ever enter his head to consider the other point of view that people also have a right to walk the streets unmolested by these often dirty and disease-ridden animals of precarious temperament? If they had seen, as I have seen, in the local hospital casualty department the badly lacerated faces and limbs of adults as well as young children, some of whom will be disfigured for life, they would realise that something must be done to protect the public and rid our streets of this menace.

The police were only carrying out their duty as requested by the school principal who has the safety of his pupils at heart. If people value their dogs and really love them, they will keep them under control.

Letters, K Lavern. Our suburb would also be improved by the temporary transfer, to it, of the police officer who removed a public nuisance and performed a public service, if only by frightening irresponsible characters into keeping their dirty, noisy, ill-trained "pets" under control.

Letters, Peter Sykes. As a visitor to your country from England, I was horrified to see your Police Force carrying pistols even on traffic duty and routine assignments.

The arming of police makes a travesty of the entire judicial system, whereby a man is considered innocent until convicted in the court of law. It automatically transforms the servant of the law into Judge, jury and executioner. A dead man, no matter how innocent or guilty, cannot appeal, and to appeal is a basic right under our penal code. Finally, is there a "watch committee" to control the behaviour of the police and, if so, what is it doing?

Letters, A Watson. It is open to doubt whether police in England would agree with the views of Peter Sykes on the question of the carrying of firearms.

To many people in this country it would be horrifying to ask an unarmed policeman to face an armed criminal, but it appears to be normal practice in England, where many police have paid for it with their lives. It is utter rubbish to claim that the arming of police (which Mr Sykes finds horrifying) automatically transforms a policeman into Judge, jury and executioner, for police here have to have very good grounds for resorting to the firearms they are called upon to use when on duty.

Mr Sykes says a dead man cannot appeal. He might have added that dead policemen cannot be brought back to life either.

Letters, B W. The carrying of pistols by policemen (very apparent with the new summer uniform) has not given me so much concern as has the apparent indiscriminate use of the pistol.

Frequently we read of police shooting at burglars and speeding motorists. While this occurs mostly in the late hours of the night, there must be a great risk of an innocent bystander or even the offender being injured, if not killed, by such indiscriminate shooting.

As it would seem to me that pistols should only be used when life is in immediate danger, the Commissioner of Police might say what are the rules regarding use of pistols; is a report furnished on each occasion a pistol is used; and what Departmental action (if any) has been taken in the last 12 months for unwarranted use of pistols?

Letters, Anti-Firearms. The question whether police should be armed, raised by Peter Sykes, brings to mind the carrying of firearms by postal officials, and its validity.

In conveying large sums of money to and from the bank, postmasters at certain post-offices are accompanied by an armed official who is supposed to walk several paces behind him. In a busy suburb it would be nearly impossible not to have one or more persons between the postmaster and the armed escort.

Should a hold-up be staged, the escort is apparently expected to use the firearm, but could he do so without killing or wounding some innocent member of the public?

It would be interesting to learn by whose authority officials are armed, and what their duties are in case of a hold-up.

Letters, Frank Snow. If "B W" and a few others writing in the same vein want to get properly on to the target of public safety, let them raise their sights beyond the Commissioner of Police and draw a bead on the Chief Secretary, who is directly responsible for the loose legislation which at present allows what is virtually an indiscriminate sale of shotguns and light-calibre rifles to anyone 16 or over.

Policemen at least get some rudimentary training in the safe handling of their arms, apart from any departmental policy as to when and where to use them. But with the right money in his pocket, any gun-ignorant, irresponsible youth can become the lawful owner of much longer-ranged firearms than any pistol, and as to how, when and where he'll teach himself to shoot is largely in the lap of the gods. Naturally, he heads for the country....for, say, a place like Robertson (rabbits, you know!)

At the last quarterly sitting of the local court of petty sessions, a week or two ago, Robertson police notched their ninetieth prosecution in the past three years against persons misusing firearms – every man-Jack of them a visiting shooter!

Apart from rabbits, Robertson district is noted for its bountiful and varied wildlife. Court records show that a dozen or so of those 90 prosecutions were for killing protected fauna. And when a policeman, in the execution of his duty, shoots a troublesome city dog, there's a regular hullabaloo!

Anyway, I'll wager my own trusty old 16-bore single-barrelled shotgun that of the 40 fatal accidental shootings in NSW in 1960 (latest available figures), not one was from a police bullet.

REMEMBER BEN CASEY

At the Annual Meeting of the American Nurses Association, **criticism was launched** against the popular TV show **"Doctor Ben Casey."** Critics said the it rarely showed nurses. **Local nurses here, at Sydney's RPA Hospital said** they liked the show. "It is over-dramatic, but who wants real life in TV". **"He is really good-looking."** "If American nurses want to see nurses, let them try to put together and sell a show about nurses."

APRIL NEWS ITEMS

Elizabeth Taylor and Eddie Fisher are divorced. This is her fourth divorce. Her previous husbands were: to the hotel heir Nicky Hilton, then Michael Wilding, and Mike Todd. The groom currently in waiting appears to be Richard Burton.

Three factory owners argued in the Arbitration Court today that their factories should be exempt from Trade Union Provisions, such as Union inspection, because **Union awards were against the will of God.** "Unionism is contrary to what God has in mind for man, and forces man onto an entirely different path from His." The factory owners were all sincere men, of good character. They would not say what form of religion they practised, though the word "Brethren" was often used. Their exemption was refused.

Australians are marrying earlier than ever before. In 1950, 7 per cent of men, and 28 per cent of women married under the age of 21. By 1960, the proportion had risen to 10 and 38 per cent. **In Tasmania, 46 per cent of girls were married under 21.** Eleven per cent of marriages were made in registry offices.

The Federal Government announced that it **was no longer necessary** for Australian citizens travelling overseas **to get a Taxation Department clearance** before being allowed to travel.

Beer in cans appeared for the first time in hotels round the nation. Price for the standard half-bottle 13 ounces will   be two shillings, which is 12 percent higher than draft beer in a public bar. Cans will be sold only by hotels and clubs and, of course, not through retail shops.

Sydney author, **Patrick White**, was awarded the **Miles Franklin** award for the best Australian novel, "Riders in the Chariot." Other books recommended included The Fringe Dwellers (Nene Gare), The Runaway (Ruth Morris), and The Good-looking Women (Ruth Park).

Attila Atalay, Mascot. "I wonder, after four years in Australia, how, when and where the average, **decent and lonely Continental single man can enjoy his elementary right to meet girls and women.**

A 20-month-old **boy drowned in a sullage pit** in the backyard of his home yesterday. The boy wandered into the backyard after pushing through a fly-screen-door. A timber cover had been removed from the pit, which contained about two feet of water.

An eight-year-old girl was hit by a train when she chased a kitten on to the line at Marayong, near Blacktown. She suffered a possible fractured skull, and was still unconscious last night. As the train approached, she crouched in the middle of the lines, but though it braked, it still hit her.

INDONESIA WAS STILL HUFFING

The problem with West Irian had not gone away. Indonesia was still claiming that the Dutch should cede the land to her. Her main real claim was that it was geographically adjacent to Indonesia proper, and might just as well belong to Indonesia as to anyone else. Certainly, on **that** argument, the Dutch had no claim at all. Then there were other arguments. One really silly one was that the people there were ethnically related to the Indonesians. To anyone with the gift of vision, that was palpably absurd. Then there were others who really believed that Might is Right, and were pretty confident that the Dutch would give up the land if its military bluff was called.

The Dutch certainly seemed to be of that mind. A few conferences of reconciliation were called, a few troops were sent from Holland, some brave statements of defiance were uttered here and there, but the Dutch were apparently not disposed to fight for the land. Given the fact that there were only about 20,000 settlers there, and that it was half the world away from the homeland, this is not at all surprising. Also, Britain and the US were not interested in being drawn into any fray, so at the end of April, **the odds** were that Indonesia would end up with the territory.

There was probably **more activity in Australia** over the issue than anywhere else. Opinions were offered often and freely. A number of commentators said that if the Indos took West New Guinea, why would they not also want the people of **East** New Guinea? Others said the matter should be decided by a plebiscite of the natives, or they argued that we would become more vulnerable to attack if Irian succumbed.

On the other hand, there were arguments that said we should cultivate and make friends with our nearest neighbours. The occasional few said it was none of our business.

Below, I have submitted just a single Letter that illustrates a few of the arguments in a reasonable way. But keep in mind that there were hundreds of such arguments, for and against, arguing for dozens of different points of views, and that really, every one of them contained **an** element of truth. It was a complete mess with every solution stemming more from individual ideology, rather than from any thought of logic. It was chaos - just like real life.

Letters, J Groutsch, Burwood. I find it strange that Mr Menzies should be so confident that all Australians will fight over Australian Papua and **east** New Guinea.

He calls anyone who would fight for **West** New Guinea a warmonger, but apparently we are traitors if we are not prepared to fight for east New Guinea – the Australian half of the island. Why the difference? Why are the people of east New Guinea so worthy of our defence and the people of West New Guinea so unworthy?

Our Prime Minister apparently enjoys the illusion that West New Guinea and east New Guinea are two quite separate and distinct countries, like two watertight compartments. He fails to see that New Guinea is one island, one country, and its people are basically one people. What is justifiable for part of the island is justifiable for the whole island,

and what affects part of the island will affect the whole island.

When the Indonesians replace the Dutch in West New Guinea – and it would be "warmongering" for Australians to attempt to prevent this takeover! – then their influence will eventually extend into east New Guinea. Any attempt to stop the advance of this influence will be as fruitless as trying to stop the advance of the tide.

If Mr Menzies thinks Australians should fight for east New Guinea (Australian New Guinea) then we should be ready to fight now – or not at all. If, on the other hand, we are to welcome the Indonesians into West New Guinea, then we should be ready to welcome their influence in east New Guinea as well.

RAPIST LAWSON FREED, THEN KILLS

In May 1954, Sydney artist Leonard Lawson advertised for a few photographic models to accompany him on a shoot in the then-remote area of Terrey Hills. Five girls were chosen and were driven to their destination. Once there, he produced a gun, tied up the girls, raped two, and molested a third with intent. They were kept in terror for the full day.

He was sentenced in June 1954 to death. But at the end of 1954, **NSW brought down legislation that removed the death penalty**. This worked to the benefit of Lawson, and his sentence was reduced to "life". A few years later, that sentence was commuted to 14 years' gaol. In early 1961, he was examined by the Parole Board, and psychiatrists, and was subsequently released in June 1961. In November of that year, he murdered a 16-year-old girl in his flat at

Collaroy. On April 5th, this year, he was convicted of that murder, and once again sentenced to life imprisonment.

Right across Australia, the news of the first rapes was sensational. Now, again, his conviction for murder was front-page news, and the tabloid papers were able to exploit the whole story for all their worth. Other papers were a bit more conservative, and the *SMH* Letters were more analytical. The first few letters below **were typical of most received**. They criticised the crime, the criminal, the Parole Board, and the system behind Lawson's early release. The last few Letters were inclined to take an attitude that showed some sympathy to the criminal.

Letters, Eric M Porter. As an ordinary citizen of New South Wales I am shocked to learn that our Government can make it possible for a man, sentenced to death in 1954 for a terrible crime, to have his sentence reduced to 14 years' imprisonment and then be released after serving only seven years of that sentence.

My horror is intensified when I realise that this step was taken in the face of the statement of the trial Judge, Mr Justice Clancy, who said, "I should not want you to leave this court in the belief that you can expect any clemency in any recommendation by me to the Executive Council. I accept the law as it is, and I think it is a proper law and a just law. I think in your case there is no reason why it should not be carried out to execution."

What system of government is it that makes it possible for some man to override the sentence of

Her Majesty's Court, especially in the face of such a clear-cut statement by the trial Judge?

I trust that the gentleman whose signature at the foot of the release signed for Leonard Lawson in 1961 suffers from remorse as he sees the result of his ill-judged step.

If this case does not convince the Government that our system of so-called "justice" needs overhauling, and inspire it immediately to undertake the vigorous reforms needed, then all I can say is "Heaven help New South Wales."

Letters, A Hutchinson. The disclosure that the murderer Lawson had already been sentenced to death for multiple charges of rape and released after only seven years has profoundly shocked the community. We have become so obsessed with the idea that such offenders are sick and can be cured and restored to the community that we overlook the natural rights of innocent people to live out their lives in safety. We have developed a group of psychiatrists who have acquired a vested interest in fostering this idea that it is the malefactor that deserves sympathy rather than the victim.

In my opinion there is only one course of action called for with proved sex offenders – and that is their castration.

Letters, Nona Frewin. Every decent Australian citizen will surely join with Mr Luscombe in demanding a public inquiry into the release of Leonard Lawson on parole after only seven years of imprisonment.

Gaol or some institution is the only place for these men, and their good behaviour in gaol should not carry much weight towards a release – after all in there they are not in contact with women and the base side of their warped natures does not assert itself.

Letters, (Dr) V Hegarty. It has long been obvious that, in its present state of knowledge, psychiatry is almost completely ineffective in rehabilitating sexual offenders, and, in the case of those whose offence has been bad enough to earn stricture from the trial Judge, completely ineffective.

While I am in complete agreement with those who deprecate suggestions of castration and flogging for sexual offenders, I urge the responsible authorities to realise that they cannot, at present be even hopeful that one sexual offence will not be repeated, after release from gaol.

Society does not hesitate to isolate lepers, as leprosy is a loathsome disease whose treatment is most protracted. Why not realise that sexual assault against others is just as loathsome, and treatment even more protracted and much less certain.

There is only one protection for society against these poor unfortunates – that is that they must be isolated, not necessarily in prison but perhaps in some form of mental hospital. The isolation must be permanent.

Judge Lloyd claims that the members of the Parole Board are highly experienced. I do not doubt this, but are they prepared to profit by their experience?

Their recent record would seem to indicate that they are dominated by that doctrinaire psychiatry which would have us believe that rehabilitation of sexual offenders is more important than the anguish of the victims and their relatives.

Enough of this nonsense! Let us realise that there are a few suffering from this incurable disease, and no matter how sorry we are for them, they must be removed from society, until such time as we can cure them.

Letters, Brian and Veronica Maltby. It is alarming how many people, as shown by letters to the "Herald," and how many Judges, by their summing up, still think of prison as a place for retribution by hard labour, scant ration and confinement. What has happened to the more humane in our population, that a mature appraisal has not yet appeared?

Prisons should be, primarily, corrective establishments for those social misfits whose confinement is a matter for quarantine until they have been successfully treated. Will some psychiatrist please emphasise the one missing fact that if Lawson had been successfully treated during his previous imprisonment, and of course he had not been treated at all, then his re-entry into society would not have caused these terrible, unnecessary deaths.

Many of the "Herald's" correspondents need to purge themselves of their own viciousness! It is a pity they do not understand that social workers, Judges, psychiatrists and prison officials could co-operate in a more productive way to pre-treat or rehabilitate those misfits who, however diseased, are also human beings.

Letters, Blessed in Anonymity. The Parole Board has been criticised and condemned in the Sydney Press recently, some people even suggesting that the board should be done away with.

I am conscious of the grief some people are experiencing at present. The Parole Board may be partly or entirely to blame for this grief.

For many years my behaviour, partly criminal, caused pain and humiliation to many people. Being unemployable for years, and experiencing a deterioration that I believe was close to automatic, culminated in my being placed in the hands of the Adult Probation Service.

Not enough am I grateful to God that this happened to me. These men were patient, tolerant, encouraging and yet firm with me. One of them in particular will never be conscious of the tremendous assistance he was to me.

While under the care and guidance of the Adult Probation Service, it was my further privilege to meet and get to know several parole officers. There have been occasions when we have tried together (not without success) to retrieve yet other men from where I was lifted – the "scrapheap" of humanity.

I hope, sir, that readers who are unable fully to appreciate my perspective will not be offended by my saying: "Thank God for the Adult Probation Service and the Parole Board."

As many of my family and relatives are living and still suffering because of my behaviour before being placed on probation, I hope I do not appear to be lacking in courage by remaining...[anonymous].

SMOKING AND CANCER

By 1962, there was generally a suspicion that smoking was bad for you. Overseas research sometimes showed a link to heart disease and lung cancer but, apart from tobacco companies who were waking up to the truth, the very real link had scarcely penetrated down to the general public.

I have include three Letters below. The first shows a revulsion to smoking, but is not in any way suspicious of the link with cancer. The second, from a more scientific viewpoint, wishes to control smoking, but not with any great sense of urgency. The third Letter is quite philosophical about the whole matter, taking the view that life is a lottery, and that cause and effect are scarcely linked.

Letters, Another Non-Smoker. Could not the hospitals themselves set the first example by barring this objectionable and unnecessary habit from a place where its practice often causes acute distress to other patients? I have myself often attempted to enter the consulting-room only to be confronted with a smoking doctor. Physician, heal thyself!

One hospital has "No Smoking" notices displayed all over the building and underneath them receptacles in which the smokers are requested to deposit their butts! Could authority command more contempt? Another has a "No Smoking" notice over the dispensary window, and through the window the dispenser, a chain-smoker, can be seen dropping ashes into the mixtures! If it is an offence under the Pure Foods Act to smoke where food is being prepared, how much more so the medicines of the sick.

The excuse that the regulations cannot be enforced is nonsense.

Letters, M Joseph, RPAH Medical Centre, Newtown. It is encouraging to see that British tobacco companies are taking steps to prevent smoking by children under 16 by removing cigarette vending machines from public places.

I was surprised, however, at statements made by spokesmen of certain Australian tobacco firms in the same context. They asserted that "the lung cancer problem is not as severe here as it is in England," that "conditions here are different," and that "this is building up into a rather stupid panic."

If we did not smoke cigarettes, the incidence of lung cancer would be only one-eighth of its present level ("Lancet," January 13, 1962). We have the knowledge and means to stop this epidemic and it surely behoves us to use them. This is not a "rather stupid sort of panic" but a reasoned and reasonable approach to a grave public health problem.

While it may not be possible to persuade the cigarette addict to forgo his habit, every effort should be made to dissuade the rising generation from beginning to smoke. This could best be done by acquainting school-children with the facts concerning smoking and of the part it plays not only in lung cancer but in chronic bronchitis and cardiovascular disease, and by the example of those responsible for their education.

There must be a change in the climate of public opinion. Tobacco companies should point out the merits of the much less harmful pipe and cigar, whose devotees rarely inhale the smoke. Local tobacco firms would do well to follow the lead of their British colleagues.

Letters, Maynard Davies. Regarding the current wave of opposition to smoking on medical grounds, may I put forward a modest dissent to the campaign of fear?

Everybody has to die of something eventually. Heart or stomach diseases due generally to rush, worry, or over-eating, kill thousands; others die of drinking too much hard liquor too often; many others are killed in motor cars or are drowned; millions of people die of malnutrition or consequent diseases; thousands of people die of cancer.

My mother died at 75 and never smoked in her life. My father, who smoked like a chimney, lived to be 90, and died in his sleep from heart failure.

On top of all this, some people live too long, dragging their weary and painful bodies into an overdue release in death. Some of these suffer mental deterioration to the point where their original personality is unrecognizable and their pointless existence a burden to themselves and others.

So what? I pray that I may not live too long, and in the meanwhile shall do what I please in moderation

– smoking, drinking, eating, motoring, swimming, to my heart's content. There is always the chance that I may die sooner than I expect. I am prepared for that eventuality.

Comment. The whole scene contrasts with that nowadays, about 2022. Most public buildings ban smoking, TVs broadcast alarming messages against its bad effects, cigarettes come in plain packaging, Clubs have separate areas for smokers, and so on. Even films and TV, which once showed heroes and heroines lounging about puffing and blowing smoke, rarely show any signs of the dreaded weed.

As I write these books, I sometimes think that in many ways, some things never change. **Not so in this case.** Over the last fifty years, smoking, as a habit, or as a vice, or as a stimulant, has moved from being a sign of sophistication down to the stage where some good-mannered people actually sniff at smokers on the fringes of restaurants. In the meantime, we are told, many people world-wide have sadly died an early death. Let's hope that the message filters through to **less-advanced countries** that are still as much at risk as we used to be.

MAY NEWS ITEMS

Olympic swimming gold medalist, **Lorraine Crapp** **(remember her?)** was admitted to Sydney hospital for a short stay last night.

Harold Holt, the nation's Treasurer, is in a fix. He announced this week that new coins would be issued to **replace the existing penny and three-pence coins.** But it could well be that the Government will soon change over to **decimal currency**, and that will mean the end of pennies altogether. **"Get your act together"** is the widespread call.

The acting Chief Secretary of Victoria, Mr R Meagher, was speaking about the problem of louts in Melbourne. He said that "it is better **to give a young man a good hiding** instead of sending him to prison, where he would associate with men worse than himself."

Mr Grant of Arncliffe writes "On visiting the Municipal Markets in Hay Street last Friday, I was shocked to see poultry dealers **wrapping live fowls in newspapers** (some in pairs) and tying them up like sausages."

Sir Alec Guinness: "Acting is an adolescent business – an indication of retarded development."

The fifth annual **North Australian Eisteddfod** will this year include competitions for aboriginal dancing and singing.

Port Moresby. A young girl had been engaged to a man from her own village, but was then **sold by her parents** to another native man from a village some miles away. The families clashed, and in **the affray, one was killed with an axe**. "He was buried for a month, then exhumed, and his skull was severed, washed, and taken to the police at a Tapini, 80 miles from Port Moresby." The killer was sentenced this week to two years in gaol.

The Federal Minister for Health announced that **the Sabin vaccine for Polio would become available soon**. It would initially be available in oral form, but plans would be made immediately for **mass immunisation**. Probably **Sabin would replace Salk** as the vaccine for use in Australia.

Charlie Chaplin will be granted a **Doctorate Degree at Oxford** University next week.

Australian military forces will be sent to Thailand. Their purpose is to **"increase stability"** in the area near Laos.

Papua prices for a bride range from two pigs in the Highlands to 1,400 Pounds in New Guinea. **In Tapina, prices range from two pigs to five Pounds in cash.**

Mrs Gerald Durrell, wife of prominent British author: "I don't want any children, and anyway, the world is already severely overcrowded without me tossing in my quota."

THE COMMON MARKET

Six of Europe's biggest nations, like France and Italy, were in the process of joining together to remove trade barriers among themselves, and to give mutual trade preferences to each other. This group was known at the time as **The Six,** and the union they ended up with is now become known as the European Common Market.

Britain was not one of The Six, but was getting very close to joining it. One of her troubles was that **her Empire already had preferential access to her markets,** and they were all afraid that if Britain joined, **then their export advantages would be foregone**. To Australia this was a very big deal, because her agricultural products had huge sales in Britain.

The Six were not keen on Australia somehow being included in their club. The British could see that they should would be better off under the new regime, but were constrained by the **concept of Empire solidarity. This was a myth** that had been badly battered during WWII, when Churchill and Britain were prepared to forsake Australia to the Japanese, in the hope that some time later this nation could be re-captured. Now, the myth was under further scrutiny. Would Britain, when faced with a choice between Empire allegiance and the Common Market, **stick with the Empire, or turn her back on it**?

This matter, now well into 1962, was occupying politicians and diplomats in many nations. Progress was slow, and the results were secretive. Britain kept on insisting that if she joined The Six **"proper safeguards"** for the empire would be set in place. But these sounded exactly like

Churchill's words during WWII, and these had been found to be worthless.

So, as the months wore on, and Britain was obviously getting closer to joining, alarm bells were here ringing louder and louder, and our agriculturalists were getting very worried. We will keep an eye on this over the coming months.

ANZUS

ANZUS was a series of treaties that bound Australia, New Zealand, and the US together into mutual defence agreements under certain conditions. Every few years the military and diplomatic chiefs for the three nations held a conference, and looked at appropriate matters. In mid-May, such a conference had just completed.

Three items of interest to Australia dominated the conference. **The first of these** was focused on Indonesia and West Irian. We wanted the US to take a stance that curbed and diminished Indonesian aspirations in the region. The American top diplomat, Dean Rusk, indicated that the US was not prepared to do this, and thus that the US would not intervene to moderate Indonesia's claims.

The second of these concerned Britain's entry to the Common Market. The US made it clear that she would not support Australia's desire to gain preferential treatment, and inter alia said that if any one was to get such treatment, then it would have to be the US.

The third of these sprang from the US's desire to see Australia play a bigger role in ANZUS. The net result was that Australia increased her aid by three million dollars, and offered a token force of military advisers to South Vietnam. She did not gain any increase in ability to influence decision-making as a consequence.

In all, the results from the ANZUS meeting were far from satisfactory. The Letters below summarised the feeling in the community.

Letters, L Ramsay. Thus, even on their "home ground," Mr McEwen and Sir Garfield Barwick have been soundly defeated by Mr Rusk, three rubbers to nil. Yet is not the United States one of the "great and powerful friends" that Mr Menzies is so fond of invoking?

In the past, whenever Australia's interests have been at stake in the field of foreign affairs, Mr Menzies or his Ministers have explained away their lack of policy by insinuating that our case is being effectively put by prevailing upon these "friends." The details of these veiled machinations are, or course, never revealed.

If the outcome of this meeting be any guide as to the efficacy of "diplomacy by intrigue," one can only conclude that this must be a dismal failure. With Britain fully occupied with Common Market negotiations, her value as a "great and powerful friend" must be rapidly decreasing. As to the United States, it is obvious that unless the policies of both nations coincide, Australia's counsel does not prevail.

The Menzies Government seems to have overlooked the obvious; whenever vital issues are at stake, the only nation with our interests really at heart is – Australia. It is our responsibility to formulate clearly our own foreign policy and to implement it within the framework of the United Nations.

Letters, W G Burulth. It has not passed unnoticed that the United States Secretary of State, Mr Rusk, on leaving Australia referred to our representatives at the ANZUS conference as **"good mates"** – as if that was how Sir Garfield Barwick and his colleagues would wish to describe themselves.

It would be rewarding to picture "Buddy" Rusk at a Press conference addressing Lord Horne or Mr Macmillan as "mates." Their lofty eyebrows would positively soar in astonishment – seeing that the appellation "mate" originated in the jargon of London's most hideously common East End costers.

Could we indulge our imagination further and visualise a typical United States diplomat walking up to the Chancellor of West Germany, and exclaiming: "Why, you old Hun, you!" or slapping France's Foreign Minister on the back with a "Hiya, Froggie!"?

Tritest of all would be hearing Mr Rusk referred to in high diplomatic circles as a "gob"!

COMMUNISM VERSUS CAPITALISM

The Reds and the Yanks were still playing that funny game, called the Cold War. Both of them were trying to show what great fellows they were, but at the same time convince the world that they were incredibly tough and invincible. So words of lasting peace, and words of atomic world wars, tumbled out in quick succession, and only one thing was certain. That was that **we** were clearly the goodies, and the other guy was bad. Just who **we** were was a bit obscure.

Right now, the Americans were showing the world their clear-cut desire for peace by exploding atoms bombs in the upper atmosphere over Christmas Island in the Pacific. The Russians were also being naughty in West Berlin where they were using their road blockade power to frustrate the Yanks. Also in Algeria, Laos, and Indonesia they were doing as much stirring as was polite to provoke the locals into fights for independence for their lands.

In the broad scheme of things, most of these activities, in one form or another, had been going on for so long that most people in Australia were not impressed. The Cold War news in the Papers was almost always on Page Three, and articles took up only a dozen column-inches. And so far this year, things had generally been pretty quite. The trouble was that both Powers had so much war equipment, and so much military man-power sitting round doing nothing, and so many ambitious politicians looking for glory, that **this current fairly sublime picture could turn nasty at the drop of a hat. Let's all hope that it doesn't.**

DUTCH NEW GUINEA

It is still there, and we are told that a couple of hundred Indonesian paratroops were dropped in Irian, and have been eaten by crocodiles, or were eating bark, or were starving to death. Maybe some of these reports are true, but in any case, the whole mess is hanging about, doing nobody any credit. I will keep the topic warm by quoting a few Letters, from writers who have all clearly adopted the Dutch cause.

Letters, Charles Huxtable. May I express through "The Sydney Morning Herald" something of the praise that is due to the Dutch, both in New Guinea and in Holland? For four years and more, they have fought a battle which concerns Australia's future more than it concerns the future of Holland. They are fighting our battle. They are upholding in New Guinea principles for which many Australians have lived and died in that country. These principles rightly belong to the United Nations, but the United Nations are too heavily involved elsewhere to do more than talk.

Holland has stood firm. Abused and insulted by her opponents, deserted by those who should be allies, pushed into the background by America, pressed by distant nations who know nothing of the matter beyond their colour prejudice, Holland has behaved with a dignity and restraint beyond all praise. Her courage and resolution have been in marked contrast to the timidity and irresolution of Canberra.

Letters, W Bacon. No one could persuade me that the Russians are helping the Indonesians to build up their armed forces out of brotherly love or sympathy, and the theory that they are gambling on the prospect of obtaining a concession on an Indonesian island for the purpose of establishing a base in the area is rather disquieting.

If this should come about, what, then, would be the value of Singapore? And what would be the use of friends in Thailand or Vietnam? They would all be outflanked. This thought brings the question of the value of a friendly East New Guinea into sharp focus. In the hands of allies, it could be the outpost of a "defence in depth" strategy for Australia and the South-West Pacific.

The United States, as leader of the Western Powers, by treating the matter as trivial, is in grave danger of once again being out-generalised by Communist strategists, as has been happening continually since the United States assumed this responsible position. Our Government, in meek obeisance, also refuses to take a firm stand when just that could make quite a difference.

In hostile hands, West New Guinea would be another Cuba – this time on our doorstep.

Letters, N Gould. Let honour be given where due. It is clear that Dr Soekarno, General Nasution and Co have made a notable contribution to the science of semantics, and the eager adoption thereof by such world figures as U Thant, Menzies, etc, clearly indicates its great linguistic and political value.

I refer to the new use of the word "negotiate," which now means: "Don't fight me – sit down at a table and **agree to whatever I say.**"

It is to be hoped a few cavilling diehards will not contest this refreshing usage when the time comes for Australia to "negotiate" with Dr Soekarno on the liberation of Dr Soekarno's blood-brothers now held in thrall by us.

Letters, H Hawkeswood,. Allow me to add one other, often forgotten, reason why Holland deserves our admiration – it was their merchant navy during those dark days of 1942-43 which brought succour to the Australian forces in New Guinea in the form of urgently needed food and ammunition. These ships, of which there were many, were practically unarmed, entirely unescorted and sailed what were then uncharted seas. Richly do they deserve Australia's everlasting gratitude.

Comment.   However, the gentleman below did not appreciate the Dutch contribution, and tells us why.

Letters, E Sturmey. Charles Huxtable is surely not serious in his remarks concerning the Dutch in New Guinea? Nevertheless, it should do no harm to assume that he is and give a serious answer.

Few would disagree that Holland has stood firm, so firm in fact as a colonial Power in the former Dutch East Indies that it has taken hundreds of years to shift her. But the Dutch still hang on in New Guinea. Millions of coloured peoples, and many whites for that matter, interpret Dutch firmness and courage as merely obstinacy and stubbornness, and as a wish to perpetuate the remnants of an empire based on white supremacy and exploitation.

Holland has had ample time to set up a Government of local inhabitants before a quiet withdrawal. That was the dignified way – as the British did in India. Had it done so, Dr Soekarno's verbal fireworks and paratroop landings would have been quite pointless now as no sane-thinking person would have classed the local people as a justifiably military target. And now the events revolving around the continued Dutch presence in New Guinea will create the most awkward and embarrassing problems for Australian trusteeship in the eastern half of the island.

We should certainly not assist the Dutch in New Guinea, but we certainly should divert all our energies to preparing the people of **eastern** New Guinea for self-government in three years or less.

WHAT HAPPENED TO CRACKER-NIGHT?

Letters, Eileen Wade, Seaforth. The permitting of the sale of fireworks so long before the day they are intended to celebrate has grown into a public nuisance so monstrous that it is surely high time the Chief Secretary took steps to prevent their indiscriminate sale.

Nobody wishes to deprive children of the joy of fireworks on the proper occasion, but the letting off of crackers of almost detonator magnitude in the streets is becoming a daily occurrence (Sundays no exception), even at night by louts returning from late shows past midnight.

Among those in my street alone, who are feeling the strain of it all, is an elderly invalid, a hospital sister, vainly trying to get sleep during the day before going on night duty, the owner of a small pet dog so unstrung and distraught that twice it has fled from home only to be found wandering in heavy traffic on the main road, trembling and too upset to even bark, a friend who all but lost control of her car when a bunger was flung under it as she was about to start from the kerb.

In order to find out what rights citizens have in this matter I have contacted my local member, Mr Douglas Darby, who informs me he brought this matter up in the House recently only to be designated "a nark and a spoil-sport" for wanting to prevent children having fun – which seems to point to the fact that the present Government has small regard for the rights and welfare of adults who simply want to enjoy peace in their homes.

A strange world indeed when adults' health is of no account because children must "have fun" when and where they wish at the expense of the community.

Letters, P Shanks.   We arrived in England on May 24, 1960 – Commonwealth Day – and to our surprise found that there were no crackers or fireworks displays. To us, this seemed peaceful and sensible, and no doubt the children of England do not miss them, having learnt not to expect them.

Letters, R Josselyn.   As one with 12 young grandchildren and wanting them to have all the fun and enjoyment I had in my young days, I wonder if, after last Sunday's experience, they will survive to fulfil my wish.

Louts (I call them this for the want of a better word) parade the streets in this area at will and delight in throwing large bungers through the windows of ground-floor flats. At 11 a.m. on Sunday two grandchildren, whom we were minding for the day, were quietly playing in the middle of the lounge-room when an over-size bunger exploded just one foot from where they were and could have blinded them.

I know little can be done to stop this hooliganism, but I suggest strongly that all headmasters of schools should lecture their pupils on the many dangers associated with crackers and perhaps prevent tragedy on May 24.

Letters, J Fuller. As everyone is aware, there will always be somebody inured, seriously or otherwise, while taking part in most forms of enjoyment. Year in, year out many are injured while enjoying such activities as boxing, football, cricket, motor-racing (even the spectator), ice-skating and "cowboys and Indians."

Are we to ban these because of a few isolated incidents? Those in favour of banning fireworks, using this argument, should be in favour of banning such things as fishing because somebody drowns now and again. Personally I enjoy watching and participating in the lighting of bungers. I see no reason why fireworks should be banned or their sale modified.

Letters, M Lukes. P M Shanks evidently was not in England in the weeks prior to November 5 when the noise of exploding fireworks was beyond anything I have ever heard in Sydney. I have not seen in this country the number of small, ragged children begging for pennies for fireworks on street corners, particularly where crowds were flowing out of the old English pubs. Nobody seemed to be concerned about this.

Letters, John Playfair. It is indeed interesting to learn, after all these years, that the letting off of fireworks in public places is unlawful under the Police Offences Act.

But surely the police can never be expected to enforce this law while sales of crackers continue unrestricted throughout the year, and with many of the "bungers," etc., containing dangerously over-large quantities of explosives. One cracker week, or two weeks at most in each year, should be sufficient for the youngsters.

The cruel effects on domestic pets should also be pointed out more forcibly to children and others. Exactly two years ago our pet dog (a pedigree female cocker spaniel, whom we had loved for over seven years) went "bush" as a result of incessant firework noises in our district. Four days later she was found dead on Pacific Highway, having apparently been run over the previous night by a car or truck. The sufferings of that poor, distracted and hungry animal during her four days and nights of wandering – before finding her final "peace" – can well be imagined.

Letters, L McCauley. Ban the teenagers from the milk bars! Ban the kids their cracker night! The knockers are at it again!

I have attended every bonfire night for 50 years at Crown Street or Palmer Street, East Sydney, one of the hectic cracker spots, and have never seen a serious accident nor damage other than burnt asphalt. Hooliganism can be found at the university, racecourses, and sporting events, but who suggests closing those avenues?

There have been 338 deaths this year in motor accidents, a great percentage caused by drunken or semi-intoxicated drivers. Has anyone suggested closing the clubs and hotels or banning liquor?

By all means curb the hooligans, but leave the kids and their cracker night alone.

Comment. Not long after these Letters were written, sales were restricted to a few weeks a year. Then the big crackers and rockets were restricted. A few years later, all bungers were taboo. Then only consenting adults could buy anything. Gradually, depending on what State you lived in, sales were limited to sparklers and throw-downs and the like.

Now we all pile into cars and drive miles in a traffic jam to watch the fireworks displays on the Sydney Harbour and the like. That is good enough fun, and every twenty years I am prepared to do it. Fortunately, I did it only a few years ago, and so will not have to ever do it again.

But cracker night, on a small neighborhood scale was great fun every year. I know it was a problem for some, in fact for many, but I often think that sensible people could have worked out a better solution than the gradual strangulation and replacement that we ended up with.

A LETTER FROM A WELL-KNOWN ACTOR

Letters, Ray Barrett, London. I am an Australian actor. I have lived in London for three and a half years amid an ever-increasing fraternity of Australian talent, all respected and regularly employed in their various sections of the arts.

Recently I had the privilege of appearing in a play by Australian Peter Yeldham on BBC television – "Reunion Day" – which was extremely well received in the United Kingdom.

I have been appalled and amazed that this play has been banned on Australian television. It is a true and honest comment on men's difficulty to settle down after the war. This is not a play attacking the RSL or, in fact, the tradition of the reunion, but a play of life. It is certainly not as described in the Australian Press "anti-Semitic, anti-Christian, blasphemous, obscene, and thoroughly nasty."

This attitude by the bigoted Australian "establishment" makes us here feel even more exiled. Drama must be truth, and I do not believe the Australian public is afraid of this. It is this attitude that has forced such great talent out of Australia. Artists are not encouraged to express themselves, make mistakes if necessary, and thereby create an indigenous drama.

How immature and insular are we? We can watch "Taste of Honey," "Irma la Douce," "Streetcar Named Desire" and say: "Well, it's not really us, is it?" - but dare to look at ourselves and we are offended. If Australians allow this attitude to persist they will surely kill anything creative in our country.

What is acceptable to the Australian "establishment"? What is the Australian writer to write about? Surely a writer must express himself the way he wants. If he must conform to subject matter non-offensive to certain sections of the community, then he must go somewhere where this attitude does not exist. This small-mindedness must stop if we ever hope to get anywhere culturally.

JUNE NEWS ITEMS

It is reported, **perhaps** correctly, that **fierce "headhunter" warriors on West Irian** have risen up against the paratroops from Indonesia. Typically, "they jump from trees onto the Indo's back, and hack him to death with large jungle knives."

Well-known writer Rachael Carlson. "Man has discovered in **powerful pest-killers** a truly frightening power **to change his world.**"

Double talk from the Brits. "We are not changing Commonwealth preferences – anyway, these preferences are changing all the time."

Cary Grant. "I do not smoke or drink, because it pleases me to stay handsome at a mature age."

Adolf Eichmann, Hitler's famous Jew-killing henchman, was executed today in an Israeli gaol.

Six players were sent off in the Rugby League match yesterday between NSW and England. They included **Ken Irvine** and **Michael Cleary** from NSW, and **Billy Boston** from England.

Athol Townley, Federal Minister: "These people (the Indonesians) who live next to us are our neighbours for **the next 10,000 years – if we last that long.**"

Five children died under tons of sand and clay yesterday when their cubby cave in a sandpit collapsed near Warren in NSW.

In a ground-breaking move, the Royal Women's Hospital announced that **husbands will in future be allowed to attend at the birth of their children**.

Sir Eugene Goossens, who conducted the Sydney Symphony Orchestra for nine years, died in Middlesex, aged 69.

TV in Oz was still **black-and-white**. Colour trialing began in 1965, but full time broadcasts did not start till 1975.

Buckingham Palace announced that the **Queen and Duke** will visit here next year. **The Tour** will take four weeks "and the announcement was received with enthusiasm in all circles in Australia".

In the last two weeks, **the US has failed in its attempts to detonate huge atomic bombs in the upper atmosphere** Mr Ecob of Pymble wrote "The reactions of the mute millions: **Thank God, they've failed again.**"

In 1972, **a mind-reader** at the Maitland Show asked me my age. I told him that **he** should be able to tell **me** what my age is. He replied that the mists were not propitious **at the moment**....

Pressing on, I told him I was 36, and he said that this was a coincidence because I would live till I was twice that, 72 years,

Can I get my money back?

BRITAIN AND THE COMMON MARKET

I would like to digress for a minute back to 1942. From Australia's point of view this was the worst year of the War. We were truly under serious threat of Japanese invasion, and our war casualties simply grew and grew and grew.

At this stage, we expected that Britain would come to our aid. We badly needed planes, tanks, guns, munitions, trained soldiers and airmen. Whatever it was, we needed it in great quantities. The Brits had been telling us for a year that if Australia came under serious attack, they would immediately send all the resources we needed.

We, foolishly, believed this. After all, the common bonds of Empire bound us to the Brits, and we had given unstintingly our manpower to the defence of Britain in WWI and, so far, WWII. Also, our shipments of agricultural products were helping Britain to avoid the starvation of Britain that Hitler hoped to achieve. Surely, now, at this time of crisis, the Brits would rally to our cause

Our **1941 Prime Minister, Bob Menzies**, kept his gloves on and lobbied ineffectually for intervention. Then our **1942 Prime Minister, John Curtin,** assisted by Foreign Minister, Doc Evatt, fought and fought with Churchill for what we wanted. For 18 months, Churchill, and his Ministers, and his Army, Navy, and diplomats all told us that help would come when needed. "Don't worry. Everything will be alright. Here's a pat on the head. Go away, and stop badgering us."

But things were not OK. Within only two months, Indo China fell to the Japanese. Then Malaya, then Singapore. Then Indonesia. At the same, the Philippines, and most islands in the Pacific. Then Darwin was bombed time and again, and Townsville, and Broome. Sydney and Newcastle were shelled by Jap subs. Australia was staring down the barrel.

Britain did not produce the goods as promised. Nothing like it, in fact. She had her fair reasons for not doing so, but the fact is that she did not do so, despite all the assurances that she would.

So back to 1962. England was about to enter the Common Market. Australia had a huge stake in this because most of our agricultural produce was pre-sold to Britain, at agreed rates that saved us from the ups and downs of foreign competition. If Britain were to enter the Market, and the Empire preference no longer applied, then the certainties of the current marketplace would disappear, and our local industries would have to bid at the lowest price that someone else might muster. In all probability, this would be a disaster for this nation.

Would Britain do this to us? Menzies, our Prime Minister, was constantly being told "Don't worry. Everything will be alright. Here's a pat on the head." Our diplomats were being told the same thing, and our Trade Department, and anyone who would listen. Certainly, Australia was putting out a tremendous amount of energy into fighting for a good deal, but it all seemed to be simply absorbed. No one would actually promise anything, and the longer the British dithered on actually joining The Six, the more likely it was that Australia would get a deal that it did not like.

Comment. In writing about this, it is all too familiar. It seems a full re-enactment of 1942. **But maybe I am**

reacting too suspiciously. Perhaps I need a cup of tea, a Bex and a good lie-down.

Below is a Letter, all the way from London, which throws a different light on Britain's current thinking. Interesting as it is, I am not too sure that some of his assertions would stand up.

Letters, Michael Rule, London. May I attempt to deflate a myth which is being fostered by certain vested interests to the effect that we in Britain are frantic to join the Common Market and are only being prevented by other members of the Commonwealth?

Public opinion polls (e.g. Gallup Poll published on March 20) prove that if it comes to a choice between the Common Market and the Commonwealth (and the Rome Treaty means we will have to choose) the British people overwhelmingly prefer the latter alternative. Also the results of all the recent by-elections show that Mr Macmillan's Government, which has not a shred of an electoral mandate to seek Market membership, has completely lost the confidence of a majority of the people.

Since her Majesty's Government has no intention of seeking the approval of the people for the devious, double-talking antics it is performing during the Brussels talks, we will yet again have to rely on the people of the Commonwealth to save the situation. We certainly hope that Mr Menzies during his London talks will defend Australian interests 100 per cent – especially as these interests coincide with ours to a remarkable degree.

Letters, G Walker. Mr Menzies' London statement that we in this country are "British to our bootheels" gave me a sleepless, soul-searching night. As a fifth-generation inhabitant, am I thus a traitor for considering myself substantially Australian?

Letters, D Maine. Menzies loves to float about London mixing with the mighty and saying all the right things, for his own benefit. If he says all Australians are British, it gets him nice warm applause, but it shows he is the wrong man for the tough talks coming up. We want a negotiator there who hits straight at our commercial interests, and does not go on with all this twaddle about Empire. That time is finished, and the sooner we wake up, the better. Send him off for home, but keep him in Ceylon for a year on the way, so he can remember what happened to our boys in 1942 when we needed them.

CAN THE YANKS REPLACE THE POMS?

If we were starting to turn away from our British dependence, could it be that our American friends would take their place? At the moment, their music and movies and dreadful clothing seemed to be very much on the upside. Below is a comment on where we were going.

Letters, I Blatchford.   I am another of the thousands of Australians who, like Claire Wagner, find almost everything American tawdry and nasty, from the brittle culture of television and rock "music" to decadence-cults and political megalomanias.

But one thing renders it very difficult to throw stones. Americans may produce all of the above, but Australians import and copy it with an avidity which seems to equate the two national spirits. In fact, the Americans can at least claim the superiority of being originators, while we merely soak up the Coke and ballyhoo like flabby sponges.

WELL, WHAT ABOUT THE DUTCH?

Our Dutch colleagues suddenly found that **our** visitors to Holland's shores would be more than welcome, and hoped that maybe such visitors would somehow generate goodwill that might be useful to them in future.

Letters, J Killen. I have been moved to write this letter by the receipt of a letter from the Netherlands War Graves Committee, and by your interest, and the Commonwealth's interest, in the West New Guinea dispute. I quote in part from the Dutch letter:

"The purpose of this letter is to make it known, that should you wish to visit the war grave of your relative buried in Holland, Reichswald or Rheinberg, the Netherland War Graves Committee will gladly welcome you as the guest of the Dutch people. This means therefore that **all transport, accommodation and meals,** while you are on Dutch soil, **will be provided at no cost to yourself**.

"Through the medium of the Netherlands War Graves Committee, the Dutch people offer you this hospitality as a proof of their great gratitude to those who, through the sacrifice of their lives, liberated the Netherlands from occupation in May,

1945, so bringing freedom back to our country. By this means, you will have an opportunity to see that the sacrifice made by British servicemen for our liberation, has not been forgotten and never will be." In the above-quoted portion of the letter the undoubted sincerity and graciousness of the Dutch people in showing their great gratitude to the people of the British Commonwealth for the sacrifices made in Holland stands out in marked contrast against the actions of Indonesia as led by its President Soekarno.

What thanks has Soekarno or any of his supporters offered to the American, the British or the Dutch for their liberation of Indonesia from Japanese control?

Letters, Margaret MacRaet. It is hard to find a piece of more confused thinking than J G Killen's letter referring to the generous action of the Netherlands War Graves Committee in inviting relatives of the fallen to visit graves under their care.

To raise the point that President Soekarno has shown no similar thanks to the Allies for liberating Indonesia from Japanese control is enigmatic. At the time of liberation, no such nation as Indonesia officially existed. It was the Dutch East Indies – **a Dutch colony** – which was liberated. Although the Indonesian people were, at this time, pressing for self-government, it was not granted until three years later. In fact, all the Indonesian people gained from liberation was the continuation of Dutch colonization and series of so-called "police actions" by the Dutch which were, in fact, armed military actions aimed at quashing their demands for self-determination.

OUR ASIAN COUSINS?

Most Australians were still not ready to accept Asians as equals. The Japanese were still reviled for the roles they had played in the War, and there were many people who would never forgive them. Other Asians did not meet the same opposition. The Chinese and Indians were remembered as having fought on our side, and had a decent public image in Australia. Though, the Chinese were a bit suspect because some of them had gone over to Communism.

There was, however, **no groundswell** for us to accept any Asians as migrants by most people. The same objections kept coming up. Not just the War-related ones, but also that they would work for half our wages, the nation would be over-run with half-casts, they would outbreed us and take over, and the list went on and on.

Still, Australians were more tolerant than they had been ten years earlier, and the pace of acceptance was quickening, and indeed it was **in the Sixties that attitudes turned round**, and we started to really remove the White Australia Policy (WAP). **Many of the changes originated in the Christian clergy**, and it is interesting to look at the **views of people on the role of Christianity.**

Letters, C Hennessey. It must be of deep concern to Australians to see the pressure of propaganda to amend our immigration laws to allow entry to Asiatics. The people mainly responsible for this agitation are religious bodies, but I doubt if their desires are promoted by Christian principles.

Do they wish to promote in Australia the conditions that are of such deep concern to Fiji, Mauritius, South Africa and, latterly, Great Britain? Do they wish to see on the outskirts of our cities areas similar to Alexander Town outside Johannesburg? – an area of broken-down slum shack dwellings peopled by ill-clad, joyless and expressionless urbanised natives, hundreds of them, unless it has been wiped out within the last few years. Can this be Christian-like? I do not think so.

In their natural habitat, although poor, they find some happiness, but in most countries predominantly peopled by whites, they are pushed aside, and the children of mixed marriages represent a greater teenage tragedy than anywhere else. To those near-white, can anything be more tragic and frustrating.

I think and I am sure every intelligent Australian must also think, that our present approach to this problem is a good one, and should in no way be amended. Certainly bring to Australian educational establishments and universities those worthy of entering the higher fields of education. They may then return to their own countries better fitted to help raise the standard of living of their own nationals. Through this, they will have gained some affection for our way of life and a knowledge of the real meaning of the White Australia policy, a policy both humane and Christian.

Letters, A D Faunce. Every country asserts its fundamental right, through its immigration laws, to preserve the racial, religious, social and economic make-up of its people.

Many Asian countries have far more rigid immigration laws than those operating here.

Australians should be eternally grateful that we, uniquely, are one homogeneous race occupying one continent. Because of this, we are free of the hatreds and internal warfare so common to other continents.

Emphatically, Asia has not run out of living room. It has scarcely touched the fringe of its development potential. With modern "know-how," Asian living standards can be rapidly raised. If we give practical help, the various Asian nations will be able to live peaceably and in prosperity within their natural religious and social groupings.

An Australian quota system for Asian migrants would simply aggravate our immigration problem. It might satisfy those few let in, but would annoy those many left out. It would prove, not our bona fides, but our hypocrisy. We intend, don't we, to preserve a nation of European origins and outlooks? If so, don't let us pretend. It won't help us in the long run.

Letters, (Rev) Gordon Powell. Developments in recent years compel me to change this view. The bitterness engendered in other countries, as in our own past, is almost entirely due to the great economic disparity between the races and exploitation on the part of whites, if not the actual practice of slavery.

More and more people are recognizing the principle, "God hath made of one blood all nations of the earth." The presence of so many Colombo Plan students has made many Australians recognise the absurdity of judging a man by the colour of his skin.

If, like Canada, we welcome cultured and influential Asians, keeping a reasonable control of the quota admitted, it would prove we are actuated by irrational prejudice. At the same time, these people would help us build such trade with Asia as could make us one of the most prosperous nations on earth, with or without the Common Market.

Letters, S Looby We are not only willing to bring "those worthy of entering the higher fields of education" to Australia; we go to these countries "to help raise the standard of living of their own nationals." This is not done with superiority, but as fellow-workers, teachers, builders, agriculturists, doctors, nurses, etc. These activities began as the work of the Christian Church and continue with, and alongside, the more recent Government efforts.

No Christian Church has ever suggested opening the floodgate of free entry to these or any other nations. We desire a controlled entry of Asians who will be absorbed into Australian communities as well as any other overseas immigrants.

CLOTHING MAKETH THE MAN

Menzies was always seen in public in a double-breasted suit with a waist-coat, of course. These suits had been forced out of fashion by shortages of material in the War, and had scarcely recovered. So to see Menzies thus dressed was something we had always been ready for. Now, our expectations were expanded, and people argued over whether this was a good thing.

Letters, (Mrs) G Jarrett. My award for the deadliest dresser for the year goes to the Minister for Trade, Mr McEwen. On Friday, when he farewelled Mr Menzies, Mr McEwen wore a suit about 15 years out of date – a laced-up, double-breasted eye-smasher with massive lapels that must have made the British Cabinet shudder during his recent Common Market visit.

Mr Townley, Minister for Defence, who also saw the PM off, appeared to be wearing a similar bow-and-arrow vintage model.

Letters, B Schumacher. Until 10 years ago a man could buy a ready-made suit in the style of his choice, but now one can only obtain a double-breasted suit **from a tailor.** Mr Menzies, the Duke of Edinburgh and Antony Armstrong-Jones, now Lord Snowdon, have often been photographed wearing double-breasted suits, showing either that the one-style fashion is not world-wide or that they can afford a tailor!

Letters, S Sanson. What business is it of Mrs Jarrett what clothes Mr McEwen wears, provided they are in accordance with police regulations?

Personally, I am tired of these "keyhole peepers" and their constant intrusion into the lives of people who are total strangers to them.

Letters, Farmer. A guinea to the hospital if Mr McEwen's double-breaster is not from Savile Row and less than one year old!

It is noteworthy that there is hardly one world-ranking diplomat – Americans excepted – who does not indulge in the correctness of a DB.

Letters, Joyce Phillips. 'No matter how old a suit is, so long as it is neat, tidy and well pressed, it looks very nice and, after all, the good or bad appearance of any garment depends entirely on the person who wears it, and not on its age or style.

Letters, G Challis. Bravo, Mr McEwen and Mr Townley. You've hastened the day I've been waiting for. I, too, have a "vintage model" "double-breasted eye-smasher" held against the day the fashion cycle would bring it "in" again. So, with great satisfaction, I'll bring it out and dust it down – and proudly wear it. So, Mrs Jarrett, don't throw out your "old-fashioned" things, just hang'em up and wait the day. They'll live again, you'll find.

THE WILD ONE

Wild singer Johhny O'Keefe was this week trying to make his fortune in Hollywood. But, others there could shout as loud as he could, and he returned to make his fame and fortune here.

JULY NEWS ITEMS

England clinched **the rubber** when it won the **Second Rugby League Test** at Lang Park yesterday by 17-10.

Rod Laver held his **Wimbledon** tennis crown by defeating Australian Noel Mulligan in straight sets.

There is a boom in the sale of **safety belts for cars**. A salesman said yesterday "Not so long ago, we might sell 10 a week. Now we sell hundreds."

A New York man lost his Court case against a major tobacco company yesterday. He had smoked one brand of cigarettes for decades, and developed throat cancer. His own doctors told him that **smoking had caused his cancer**, but opposing corporate doctors disagree. It was held that, in this landmark case, there was **insufficient scientific evidence to reach a decision.**

Four Japanese warships have arrived in Sydney on a goodwill tour. As the ships arrived at Sydney's Garden Island, a band on their flagship played "Waltzing Matilda" and "A Life on the Ocean Waves." Rear-Admiral Nagai said he wanted "to **improve our traditional friendly relations between the countries**. I believe the majority of Australians are friendly to us now. **The war is over.**"

A distinguished British scientist wrote in a prestigious Journal that **he expected a cure for cancer within 20 years.**

Women tea-makers in NSW offices will soon be unionised. All women who make tea in offices or factories will be forced to join. **Billy- boy**s who make tea for men on outdoor work are currently covered by a different Union, and the two Unions have agreed not to poach members. The office tea-ladies will seek an award providing **annual leave, long-service leave and sick pay.**

Lake Macquarie Council Library (NSW) will place all **books containing four-letter words in a special section** of the library. A spokseman said that this section will probably be the busiest in the library.

The **Federal Minister** for Air, Leslie Bury, put the cat among the pigeons by saying that if the Brits **did** join the Common Market, **it would be no big deal for us.** In fact, it should wake us up to go and **chase more profitable markets.** Stop fooling ourselves; the Brits would in the long run do what was **good for them**, and the thought of them looking after **Australia's** interests was silly....

The Oz hierarchy had a fit. Here was a man saying, out loud, things that they were hoping to keep to themselves. So, denials, rationalizations, scorn, and bitterness all poured out in quantities. After a few days, **Mr Bury was sacked.** But some of the nation's vested interests realised that **reality would soon to be upon them.**

A QUICK LOOK AT CHURCHES IN 1962

It's about time I had a quick look at some aspect of Church life. Really, for a reader such as myself who is concentrating on daily papers and Magazines and the like, it is easy to forget the Churches still played an important part in the lives of the community. Their trouble was that they were no longer in the news. Twenty years ago, at the height of the War, many people were turning to them for solace. Ten years ago they were forceful in telling everyone how they should restructure society. **Now**, they seemed to have retreated, to have gone out of society, and back to their faithful in the congregations. There were a few firebrands still being heard on social issues, but these were the exception.

Letters, W Lawson. I cannot allow the somewhat blighted view of your correspondent, W W F Pratt of Parkes, that "the Church is at the point of death," to pass unchallenged.

For most thinking people the threat of nuclear war is not wreaking spiritual devastation but surely turning people's minds toward the basic teachings of the Christian Church. I am certain more and more people are seeking the comfort and guiding light of the Christian way of life for this very reason.

As to Mr Pratt's indignation that the church directs attention to the needs of teenagers by giving rock 'n' roll services, billiards and Barney's Clubs, has it not always been the policy of the Christian to take the Gospel to the people wherever they may be? The Church is surely the more worthy of praise for rising to the occasion and adapting the

Christian teaching to the needs of the young and taking the Gospel to the places of entertainment for teenagers.

Letters, Tom Smith. Mr Lawson misses the point, as almost all clergy do nowadays. It feels good to get teenagers together for a few hours and help them to entertain themselves. But Police Boys Clubs do that, equally well. It is not necessary to fill them with silly talk about the love of God.

What is needed is some straight-talking agency that will discuss the ethical and moral dilemmas everyone is faced with every day. For young people, the prime candidate is sex. For middle age people, it is infidelity and cheating on your spouse. For the elderly, it is the problems of chronic illness and the certainty of death.

This is hardly a syllabus, but it gives you the idea. But discussions of these matters need to be bold and shocking, full of daring arguments from all sides of a question. I won't presume here to nominate who the various instructors should be, but there is no way a clergyman can have the life experience to be the instructor. They should keep right out of it all, and keep God out of it too.

People today do not need the Bible and religion. They need insight into all those taboo topics that the churches wrap in velvet, and pussy-foot round. Once a Church establishes it is a place for straight talk, people will come back again and again, and straight talk will do away with the mealy-mouthed rubbish that is talked today.

OH GOODY. A ROYAL TOUR NEXT YEAR

I must say that the Queen and I have never met up. Somehow, our schedules have always been too busy, and the fact that she has spent much of her life 12,000 miles away has contributed. In any case, I must say that I quite like what I have seen of her over eighty years, and I admire her greatly for doing a very difficult job so very well. Even **the monarchy** I don't mind, and would like to stick with it until something better comes along. So, basically, I can take her or leave her, and the thought of a Royal Tour has always been very ho-hum to me.

Not so for many, many other people. The coming visit evoked strong reaction, but – like a debate about changing our Constitution and form of Government – there was no sign of unanimity.

Letters, H Parkster. Emphasis should undoubtedly be placed upon ordinary folks having the greatest access to the Royal presence during the coming tour by the Queen and the Duke of Edinburgh. In this regard, no better choice of people for Royal patronage could be made than to follow the traditional patterns established over the years on Royal tour occasions.

State Government, Lord Mayors, district committees, etc., and all their familiar cronies could surely be relied upon to provide a bevy of as **ordinary** a bunch of Australians as any Royalty could wish to meet.

Letters, Advance Australia. As six young working women, we would like to know why we are supposed to be so thrilled with the forthcoming visit of the

Queen. Also, what gives our civic leaders the right to speak (without any previous consultations) for "the whole of Australia"?

We are not at all thrilled, and there must be many other people thinking along these lines. In times like these, when there is insufficient money for so many essential developments in Australia, the cost of such a visit to the Australian public must far outweigh anything to be gained.

In any case, with Great Britain moving towards entry into the European Common Market, and the expense of Commonwealth trade preferences, it seems incongruous, to say the least, that we should be expected to cheer loudly at "this further strengthening of Commonwealth ties." Apparently Mr Menzies and our civic leaders are unaware that, in fact, these ties are already on the way to becoming irrevocably untied.

Let's keep our sense of proportion in world affairs. If the Commonwealth is coming apart through Great Britain's committed policy in Europe, then not all the Queen's visits or all the Queen's men can put it together again.

Letters, P Richardson. The Territory of Papua and New Guinea is one of the few outposts of the British Commonwealth which has not been graced by a visit from her Majesty Queen Elizabeth II.

From the Papuan point of view, the remoteness of the Queen, a figure familiar to all who attend meetings of native local government councils where her portrait is ever displayed behind the rostrum, would be removed and her Majesty would become a reality.

At present there is still a feeling among the more educated natives that it is a good thing to be part of the British Empire "whatever it is."

While there is every hope that the Queen's visit will strengthen Australian ties with Britain and awaken latent patriotism, a new field awaits her in the north, one smaller in population but greater in challenge for the future.

The Duke of Edinburgh's visit in 1956 may well preclude the territory from the itinerary for the forthcoming Royal visit, but the desirability of a Papua-New Guinea visit should be kept in mind.

Letters, G Sheen. Are we so impoverished by world standards, or so miserly and boorish, that we cannot welcome with good grace such distinguished guests who are doing us the honour of visiting us?

Private firms contribute substantially to the cost of decorations, and the pageantry and gala atmosphere brings brightness and excitement into many otherwise dull and lonely lives.

Furthermore, why involve our Queen in the Common Market wrangle? She is our Queen, too, and surely we do not choose our guests solely for what they can do for us.

Letters, Joyce Paterson. No one could admire and respect the Royal family more than I do, but when our civic leaders speak for the "whole of Australia," I agree with "Advance Australia" that it is a bit much. We are never under any circumstances asked our opinion about the advisability of spending such a vast amount of money; nor do we know, until we read the Press, whether the presentation took the form of a diamond wattle, koala or boomerang – it's all done with mirrors!

Letters, A Wilkinson. It's pretty evident why "six young working women" hide behind the pseudonym "Advance Australia." This country has advanced only because the majority of its people have inherited from their British ancestors the priceless gifts of loyalty, sincerity, decency and logical reasoning.

Letters, F Teague. H Parkster's sarcastic letter re "ordinary" people is typical of those who take no part in public life and mock those that do. Do we want ordinary or superior people to look after ordinary affairs? I think the former.

Comment. These Letters, and many others, revealed the division in society over the Common Market deliberations. There was a body of people, about half perhaps, who wanted us to be tied, in all things, with Britain. That means Empire, monarchy, trade, culture, and sport, and all else. Most of these people would have been born in England, or be first generation Oz. It would not matter to them – at a distance – if the British had to pay a few pence extra for Oz butter. **The Empire and all that** were worth the cost.

The other group, probably younger, were saying that our ties with Britain were an illusion. No false sentimentality for bygone days here, just harsh economic reality. Go out and sell to the highest bidder. Even if he is Asian.

Second comment. It is interesting to note that even in the **year 2021**, there is still a large rump of Anglo-philes in this nation. Of course, you saw this in the defeat of the Constitutional Amendment that sought to introduce a Republic a few years ago. You can see it in the excitement, in some sections, that is always still generated by a Royal Tour.

Still, it is hard to see this continuing for many more decades into the future, given the fact that our migrants are now coming mainly from non-British countries, and given that our younger folk have few direct ties with Britain. Some of us older folk, who at one time gloried in the splendid vision of **pink all over the map** of the world, will have to accept that, for OZ, perhaps, **there won't always be an England.**

MORE ON CONTRACEPTIVES

Contraception issues still stirred Letter-writers. I have included three Letters that touch new ground.

Letters, Pharmacist. In your columns you report the arrival in Australia of a medical specialist who has been engaged to deliver a series of lectures on the use of oral contraceptive pills, for the Sydney University's Post-graduate Medical Committee. The report also states that Dr Swyer's visit is being sponsored by the drug company A G Schering Ltd.

It may be pertinent to ask whether the ethics of the medical profession have so deteriorated over the past few years that we have the spectacle of a medical specialist being imported by a post-graduate body for the purpose of boosting the use, and naturally furthering the sales, of a patent and proprietary medicine.

The firm of A G Schering Ltd, which is sponsoring the specialist, is the manufacturer of the most popular brand of oral contraceptive pills.

Surely this is a most serious departure from the original code of ethics as laid down for the profession, which, after all, has enjoyed a great deal of protection as a profession, and must therefore keep to the original high ethical standards if it is to retain the confidence and respect of all concerned.

Letters, John Maguire. If oral contraceptives are "sales-pressured" on to the community and, in turn, widely used, I venture that future generations will judge us most harshly.

This country, which is so dear to us all, needs to be developed and developed quickly! This fact necessitates a vastly increased population; and, with due respect to the magnificent contribution of our immigrants, whose countrymen we must attract in every-increasing numbers, the native Australian does not have to go through a difficult assimilation process with all its trials and difficulties.

We will lose our Australian characteristics to an unnecessary degree, as it will be necessary to attract more migrants in order to fill the unnatural void. We will become a nation of old people; our social services will be strained to the limit, to the detriment of the economic growth of the country, and hardships will result on the people themselves.

Letters, I Edwards. The new contraceptive pills are now probably the most frequently prescribed method of contraception, and it had been confidently expected that the present huge sales of these pills would result in their cost falling to a level readily afforded by most people.

The manufacturers have indeed been able to reduce the price greatly, but simultaneously the Federal government has seen fit **to impose last month a sales-tax of 25 per cent** on these preparations, the maximum rate at which any pharmaceutical item is taxed, and this is paid irrespective of whether their use is to be contraceptive or strictly therapeutic. This is the first and only time sales-tax has been applied to any restricted drug (any drug for which a prescription is required). The 25 per cent tax is also levied on other contraceptive preparations.

The conclusion to be drawn is that the Government wishes to discourage the use of contraceptives. If so, it should say so. It should be prepared to justify itself before the electors, rather than by sneaking in the imposition of maximum sales-tax under cover of a manufacturers' price reduction.

It should also be asked to justify the taxing of already expensive drugs widely used in the medical treatment of conditions such as functional uterine bleeding and endometriosis, where such treatment is often the only alternative to major surgery.

Comment. One question I did not address, due to space considerations, was one which Letter-writers mentioned often. The question was whether Catholic doctors could or should prescribe the Pill for patients, Catholic or otherwise. Many of them were in a moral bind, caught between the teaching of the Church and the ethics of their profession. And their Catholic patients were also in a bind, as to whether to switch doctors, or whether to conform, if they were refused the Pill. All I can say here is that there were dozens of different stances, and a large number of very disturbed people, and no single dogma or view dominated.

GOV'T SUPPORT FOR PRIVATE SCHOOLS?

Ever since Federation of Australia in 1901, Australia had been vexed by controversy over the place of private schools in our education system. These schools, the vast majority of them being Catholic, provided a nation-wide network of primary and secondary schools that **paralleled** our system of State schools.

Arguments over the years had come and gone, but generally the opponents of Government funding for private schools decried them because of the cost of running a second system, and because taxpayers were required to subsidise religious training. Also, many people resented them as part of Protestant-Catholic enmity that permeated society.

Proponents of the Catholic schools argued that State schools did not provide the religious education and atmosphere that was needed. Further, that Catholic parents paid taxes as well, and why should they support a State system that did not give them what they wanted? Why should they pay for two systems? And they generally closed their argument with the pragmatic advice that **if the Catholics closed**

down their schools, the existing State schools would not be able to cope with the influx of Catholics.

But these mainline arguments represent **only a fraction of those advanced.** Over the years, there were hundreds of different points of view presenting the best that **logic and mutual bigotry** could devise.

The Bishop of Goulbourn. In mid-July, **the cat was placed among the pigeons.** The Catholic hierarchy announced that all Catholic schools in the City of Goulburn would be closed for six weeks starting from the next Monday. It said that students would be directed to Public Schools, and if some students could not be accommodated there, then they would be kept at home. There were six schools involved, some of which had boarders, and their total enrolment was 2,200 students. A meeting of 500 parents had approved the closure.

The initial Government estimates were that the Public schools could take about half of these and that the other half would be turned away.

The Government, though, reacted with great caution. It made it clear from the start that it would not get involved in slanging matches between the various combatants. This was hardly surprising. After all, at the last election, it had campaigned **against** State Aid. **On the other hand**, Catholics made up more that a quarter of the total number of voters and when roused, they would vote as a bloc. Beware the crouching lion.

The effect on **correspondence to the newspapers** was beyond belief. The *SMH,* for two weeks had problems with culling Letters down to a printable mass. For example, on July 13, (and subsequent days) the Editor wrote:

Public interest in the controversy over the threatened closure of Roman Catholic schools in Goulburn from next Monday continues unabated. Rarely has the Herald received so many Letters on a single subject. Lack of space precludes the publication of more than a small selection.

I too have a lack of space. All that I can present **here** is a very small sample, some of them just extracts from much longer Letters.

Letters, W Johns. All other considerations apart, the action in Goulburn is as significant as the fight of workers in earlier times for understanding of their unity and demands for wage justice.

Roman Catholic parents of Goulburn are to be congratulated on their courage, and let us hope they are instrumental in demonstrating to the public the validity of their claim, which, after all, is for the welfare of Australia and its citizens.

Letter, K Quinlan. The planning of the Department of Education is based on the assumption that it will have to provide for only three-quarters of the children in any area. The whole program of the system – buying land, building schools, training teachers – is built on this assumption.

The Roman Catholic and other independent schools are partners with the State schools in educating our children to a common scholastic standard. Is it fair that only one of the partners is given all the income when a proportionate share should be given to each?

Letters, A H Ramsay. It is absurd for Roman Catholics to argue that the crisis is due to double taxation. The facts are: Roman Catholics are taxed once – in the same manner as every other taxable person – for the upkeep of public utilities and institutions. Any money a Roman Catholic pays for the support of his church school is a contribution to his Church, since the school is an inseparable part of it; it is certainly not a tax, but a self-imposed (or hierarchy-dictated) burden.

Letters, John Watsford. Once again the ugly question of State aid for Roman Catholic schools has come forth for airing. If Roman Catholics insist on having their children having a religious education, then let them pay for it. I can't recall every having heard similar demands for State aid from other religious bodies, but the same conditions apply to them.

I insist that any taxes go towards State education without the religious indoctrination (when the Communists do it, it is called brain-washing) that the Roman Catholic institutions indulge in.

Letters, David Scarlett. The decision to close Roman Catholic schools in the Goulburn area in an attempt to force state aid for denominational schools is deplorable. In New South Wales there is a perfectly good system of free education along Christian lines. However, because a minority in the community wants something extra, the taxpayer is expected to subsidise denominational schools. If the Roman Catholics in the Goulburn area cannot afford to send their children to a Roman Catholic school, let them go to a State school. If they want something extra let them pay for it.

Letters, Bernard O'Donnell. The "Herald" describes the action of closing the schools as "political blackmail", when, in fact, the citizens of Goulburn are merely exercising their civic rights as citizens of New South Wales in demanding free education for their children as laid down by Act of Parliament. Blackmail is a crime. Is this then a crime? They are not demanding money with menaces – they are asking for justice for justice's sake.

Is it unreasonable for the State Government to have to cater for a six-week emergency, when education is supposed to be free for all children at State schools? How much more of an emergency were all Catholic schools to close overnight and if the burden of educating these 170,000 children were thrown in to the lap of the State Government!

Where would the "Herald" or the Government find the 400 million Pounds suddenly needed to build, staff and furnish the new schools? Where would the extra thousands of teachers suddenly appear from?

It is quite obvious therefore that the "well-developed but perennially hard-pressed secular education" in this State could not cope with such a sudden influx of 170,000 children. Would it not be easier to provide some means of support such as is provided by the British Government to all the schools in England, including the schools for the five million English Catholics and the schools of the tens of millions of English Protestants?

Letters, D O'Neil. So somebody has finally found enough gumption to protest publicly about the Government's hide-and-seek policy regarding financial aid for Catholic schools. I have three sons attending a school where there are eight lay teachers whose salary is paid by the parents of the pupils. If Catholic schools were closed, these eight and thousands of other teachers would have to be paid by the Government. This fact, in itself, should make certain narrow-minded members of the community realise that requests for assistance are not unreasonable. I sincerely hope the Minister for Education will be a lot stronger on this issue than some of his colleagues have been in the past.

Letters, Dorothy Koonin. This claim by the Roman Catholic Church and its adherents that because they pay taxes, so much should be returned for their schools, is constantly recurring. (I understand no taxes are paid on their substantial properties.)

I too, a non-Catholic, have been paying taxes for many years. Since I have never had any children, can I claim exemption (and thousands like me) from paying my share towards the education budget? Further, since the Roman Catholic Church positively forbids birth-control, why should those who exercise it (with a view to a better standard of living for all concerned) be penalised to pay for those who, by their own actions (or lack of them), find themselves with heavier expenses than they like?

Letters, F Judson. Whichever way you look at it, using children as a strike weapon is despicable.

Comment. On the next fateful Monday, the Public schools accepted all but 300 students in a well organised manner. During the week, no incidents of animosity between students were reported. At the end of the first week, the Bishop called off the "strike", and Catholics returned to their own schools the following week.

Both sides could, if they so chose, look with some satisfaction at the result. **The State** showed that, if given a little more time, it might just cope with the numbers displaced from Catholic schools. At least in some areas. **The Catholics** delivered a message, heard across the nation, that they were getting serious about State aid, and were now determined to force Governments to legislate for it.

AUGUST NEWS ITEMS

There are 13,600 persons recognised as **aborigine** in NSW. Of these, 235 are described as **full-blooded**.

An Italian seaman, Mario Ricelli, **met and married a Japanese woman in 1950 in Japan.** He saw her every three months when his ship returned to Japan. He officially migrated to Australia in 1956. He then **had to wait five years to become naturalised.** He did that a few months ago, and so now, his wife, and 10-year old daughter, can come and live in Oz. **They did that this week.**

The first Court cases on the drug Thalidomide were being heard. In London, 1,000 women were awaiting a finding on a woman's claim that the drug caused her to **give birth to a seriously deformed baby.** Many more cases would be decided over the next few years.

Marilyn Monroe died this morning (Aug 5th) from an apparent overdose of barbituates.

Russia lanched two separate manned space craft today. This is the first time that **two** men have been in space at the same time.

The cost of building the Sydney Opera House has blown out from the **$4.8 million estimate in 1960**, to the **current actual figure of $12.5 million.** The work is not **scheduled** to finish **until 1965**, so there is scope for further increase over the next few years.

Australia's Minister for External Affairs, Sir Garfield Barwick, said that he had been told by Indonesian Dr Subandrio that **Indonesia had no claim or designs on Australian territory** in New Guinea. Mr Subandrio might in time prove to be telling the truth, but commentators said that Barwick was **being very naïve** accepting this info at face value.

Lieutenant-General Gordon Bennett died on August 1st. After a distinguished military career, he was much remembered because he had been Commanding Officer of Australian troops when **Singapore fell to the Japanese in 1942**. He escaped to Australia. There were very many people at home who argued that he should have stayed with the 15,000 Australian troops who were captured and sent to Changi for the duration.

Bennett was given a full military funeral in Sydney, with 5,000 mourners packing the Town Hall, and another 10,000 lining the route in George Street.

Author J B Priestley on Britain's (and Australia's) **entry to the Common Market**. "We shall have to outwit and outsell a crafty rabble of West Germans, French and Italians, with not a **title or decent ribbon among them.**"

The Federal Member for North Sydney, **Billy Jack, this week made a speech in Parliament.** It was his fourth speech since he was elected in 1949. At the conclusion, a full House cheered him and slapped him on the back.

AGREEMENT ON WEST IRIAN

The Dutch and the Indonesians, under the auspices of the UN, reached an agreement on the future of New Guinea. The Dutch would gradually withdraw over a period of about two years, and hand over the administration to the Indos. Some property necessarily forfeited by the Dutch would be compensated for, and Dutch settlers could choose to stay or go. The military protection of the half-island would become the responsibility of the Indonesians, who would also now have the right to tax the inhabitants, and the duty to provide services. Self-government should be an option within ten years. On the face of it, the agreement reached seemed a thoroughly civilised one, one that had been worked out between equals without duress or panic.

There were pockets of strong opposition to all this here in Australia. Foremost among these was the *Sydney Morning Herald.* This newspaper published a number of Editorial comments, and dozens of Letters that ripped the agreement to shreds. It argued that Australia should have intervened diplomatically, and that **in the last resort, we should have gone to war to protect our various interests.** It said that we would soon have problems along our border with Papua, that the Indonesians were now on an expansion path southwards to Australia, and that the Russian Reds had moved much closer to Tasmania, which as we all know, was their ultimate goal.

Letters poured in to the *SMH.* Most of those **published**, not surprisingly, supported the Herald's cause. A sample of these Letters is given below.

Letters, (Canon) G O'Keeffe. Thank you, indeed, for your very powerful and moving editorial, "Aggression Proclaimed Respectable." One feels ashamed that Holland was thus forced into the position of allowing her West New Guinea people to be now governed by Indonesia.

What hope, after Indonesian rule, even if it is written on United Nations paper, will they have of choosing their ultimate freedom? They have, indeed, been thrown to the wolves and the Communist front thus brought on to Australia's very doorstep.

One feels proud that the "Herald" has championed the cause of these west Papuans and shown to the world the pathetic weakness of the Australian Government.

Letters, Ralph Randell. With the conclusion of the Indonesian-Dutch agreements on West New Guinea, Australia's prestige falls to an all-time low. Or rather the prestige of our leaders – for none seemed to raise a voice in protest.

A world which once looked upon the Atlantic Charter – with all its legal weakness – as a new path for human endeavour to follow should stand aghast at this cowardly betrayal of the Papuan people who live in the western end of New Guinea, particularly when United Nations pundits are screaming their heads off for immediate self-government and independence for the same race in eastern New Guinea. Free one lot; enslave the other!

Surely, soon the people of the United States will squirm when they learn to what depths their political leaders have fallen by this betrayal, not only of the simple Papuans but of the high principles the American people initiated when they asked that colonization of any race by another should vanish from the earth.

Letters, E Perks. As a fourth generation Australian, I have always been very proud that this nation has never in the past been intimidated by any country, either Asiatic or Western, that cared to rattle the sabre. It is this background that our great tradition of Anzac has come from.

What is the position now that the Government has been frightened by threats of war by an Asiatic Power to forsake an ally and friend of this country, namely the Dutch?

It is so contrary to the past tradition of the Anzac spirit, which has done so much to form the Australian way of life!

Letters, Lawrence Tabihula, Port Moresby. I am one of these primitive Stone Age Papuan animals. I used the word "animals" because the United Nations and the USA has just traded half of us to Asia like cattle. Maybe some Australians do not know that this West New Guinea border is only a line on a map and the same animals live both sides of it. When will they sell out this half?

Once upon a time we were not animals, but fuzzy wuzzy angels, but that was long ago when the Americans and Australians were fighting Asians and needed our help. We are thankful to Australia for what she has done here since the Pacific War. Some of us animals have been taught to read a bit, and we would like to say this. Thank you to your newspaper for telling the Australian people that a great crime has been done.

Secondly, this United Nations is now clear to us as a cooperative society of cheats and liars that only hears the voices of the people when the language is Asian. We are telling our people not to have anything to do again with the United Nations visiting missions. Alright, we are animals and animals cannot talk, but some animals in the bush are dangerous.

To us simple Stone Age Papuans without intelligence, Japs and Javanese look the same and we think they act the same and can die in the bush the same. We are thinking that it won't be long now before we are fighting Asians again and I am remembering that Jap dysentery killed half my village and Japs killed my father with bayonets for helping American airmen.

The Government took the position that the whole matter was none of its business. It said that it was up to the Dutch and the Indonesians to find a successful formula, and they had done that. They argued further that Indonesia had no designs on east New Guinea, and the Communist menace was of no consequence.

A few published Letters supported the Government.

Letters, (Dr) John Child. I see the agreement between Holland and Indonesia as the belated fulfillment of the understanding, reached at the time of Indonesian independence, that control of West Irian would be transferred to Indonesia. Dutch intransigence and their dishonourable attempt to avoid fulfilling their obligation have, over the years, provoked the Indonesians to direct action.

In my opinion the Indonesians have shown commendable restraint in the face of Dutch provocation. Furthermore, the alleged Dutch concern for the rights of the Papuans has a hypocritical ring. For centuries they almost completely ignored the Papuans, preferring to concentrate their energies in exploiting the wealthier islands of Indonesia.

Finally, is **Australia's treatment of the aborigines**, or the natives of eastern New Guinea, such a model of perfection that we can afford to condemn, in advance, the Indonesian treatment of the Papuans in West New Guinea? Your jingoistic exhortations and the implication that Australians should have been prepared to go to war over West Irian seem to me unrealistic, prejudiced, and irrational.

Letters, S Lipscomb. At last, West Irian will be given to those to whom it rightfully belongs. Still the "Herald," the Colonel Blimps, and the old-world reactionaries continue to bleat. Perhaps one of these days they will realise that this year is 1962 and not 1862.

The postwar years have seen the rise of Afro-Asian nationalism, which is transforming the world for the better.

Comment. Four weeks after the agreement was announced the *SMH* was still working hard on the issue. Despite that, the generally accepted view was that the Government had been correct, and that we had no right to intervene in the matter. That is not to say that some of the views supporting a stronger stand were not valid, it is just saying that, on the balance, we were better off accepting the Government's stance.

Looking back from the year 2021, it turns out that many of the fears raised were not to be worried about. The Indonesians in general have been good neighbours, they have not shown desires to take over East New Guinea, and they had not acted as a conduit to Communism. Certainly, Australia did not suffer the **strong alienation from Asia** that would have come if we had supported the **colonial Dutch** against **an emerging Asian nation**. In all I have to say that the Government did the right thing here.

ABORIGINES' BETTER DRINKING

The NSW Cabinet approved legislation to enable all aborigines in the State to drink alcohol without restriction. About 1,100 of them could already do so, because they had applied for and received an exemption certificate that allowed their drinking. However, with the new legislation, all the remaining 12,500 would be able to do so, without a certificate.

A number of country hotel-owners reacted over the next few days. Many of them were negative. They said that the main reason for their objection was the adverse reaction of their white customers to the new laws. A manager at Lismore said we will not serve aborigines partly because of the existing customers' reaction, and partly because of aboriginal behaviour. At Casino, the comment was "My customers have said they will go elsewhere if there are any aborigines here. They do not want them in the bar breathing over their shoulders."

On the other hand, a publican at Cowra said "the customers will be quite happy to see the aborigines come in. We always feel sorry to see them hanging round, and not being allowed to come in because of their colour. I do not think they will go mad. They will settle down after a couple of weeks."

Mr Michael Sawtell was the most persistent correspondent that the *Herald* had. Since the War, he had been on the Board of the NSW Aborigines Welfare Board, and in that role, had been ceaseless in pursuing the welfare of aborigines. His views were generally controversial enough to get about one hundred of his Letters **published**, so it was not at all surprising to find he had something of interest to say now.

Letters, Michael Sawtell. Now, after the news of a brawl of drunken aborigines at Tabulam, perhaps more notice will be taken of my views about the evil of drink among our aborigines.

The decision by State Cabinet to lift Section 9 of the Act to give all persons of aboriginal blood an "open go" to drink was only made to appease the city theorists and pressure groups. Four members at least of the Cabinet are against this "open go."

The aborigines owe the Welfare Board 64,000 Pounds for back rent on their 17/6 houses. Last year, 8,175 aborigines were arrested for drunkenness, some of them with 20 and 30 previous convictions. I was a member of the Board for 18 years, so I know the facts.

There is little or no social drinking among aborigines. **They drink to get drunk and then fight.** That is their form of amusement. Any decent well-behaved aboriginal can go into a hotel and drink, and the police and publican will shut their eyes to the strict letter of the law. Let it stay at that. The moral problem that goes with drunken aboriginal women in unspeakable.

Comment. Mr Sawtell's views always elicited strong responses from other *SMH* readers. In this case, the Chairman of the Aborigines Welfare Board, where Sawtell had previously pontificated for years, took up the task.

Letters, A Kingsmill, Aborigines Welfare Board, Sydney. It is clear from the figures that, despite the prohibition on the supply of liquor to aborigines not exempted from the Act, there were many people quite willing to supply them with alcohol, generally of an inferior kind. Mr Sawtell says there is little or no social drinking among aborigines. If the law was observed, there should have been very little of any kind. The illicit circumstances in which this form of "sly grog" has been carried on certainly has not made for any form of social drinking.

Letters, Desmond Merkel. Now that a more enlightened community is moving to abolish the restrictions on the supply of alcohol to aborigines, it is appalling to read that some publicans may refuse to serve them. No doubt a number of aborigines will misbehave when allowed into hotels. What else can be expected when we regard the conditions under which we force them to drink? Because of the law now to be repealed, the aborigines have to buy their liquor illegally and secretly and drink it in the same shameful secrecy. Unscrupulous publicans and others supply them with the rawest and most potent wines at exorbitant prices. Because the law forbids liquor, no effort has been made, or could be made, to teach aborigines the proper approach to alcohol.

The belief that there is something in the physical constitution of the aboriginal which makes him peculiarly susceptible to alcohol is without foundation. It is one of the many myths cherished by ignorant whites to justify their treatment of a coloured minority. Any publican refusing to serve aborigines would be setting himself against the manifest wish of the Government and the community. Such irresponsibility might well be considered by the Licensing court on applications for licence renewals.

If some of the aborigines misbehave, the publican has his remedy. The real advantage, of course, is to the younger generation aboriginal, who now will be able to buy a beer in a hotel when he wants it, instead of gulping heavily fortified wines in secret.

TRIVIA GALORE

It's about time we had a real dose of trivia. Of course, the writers generally did not think of them as such but, looking back, it is hard to take some of them all that seriously.

Letters, C Walker. Telstar space flights and rockets to the moon leave me unimpressed. For sheer ingenuity I nominate the machine which pre-packs meat and bacon rashers in cellophane.

With fiendish cleverness, it can tuck out of sight scrap odds and ends to make weight.

Letters, Ion Idriess. Hope I'm not lumbering in where "angels fear to tread," but the article "camels' blood may help in merino breeding" intrigues me because it says that "the camel, apparently, does not harbour ticks, because not one was found on any of the 65 camels shot."

Could this possibly mean that the blood of "local" camels, at least, contains some deterrent, probably a poison, against ticks? If so, doubtless the expedition has realised that it has a chance of "killing two birds with one stone" – obtaining its objective of a breed of **drought-resistant sheep** by virtue of the "drought resistance" in these camels' blood and the breeding of **tick-resistant cattle**.

As we all know, the tick, with its fever and allied ills, yearly plays havoc among our Northern Australian cattle herds.   Australian has lost hundreds of millions through the tick.

So if scientists, through the miracles that we now know are contained within blood, could develop **a breed of drought-resistant sheep and tick-resistant cattle**, they would accomplish one of the greatest among the great feats of science – and would give an extraordinary and lasting impetus to the development of our continent.

Letters, Douglas Anderson. I wonder if you have noticed that the serial number of the "Herald" jumped from 38,889 on August 9 to 38,900 on August 10, 38,901 on August 11 and 38,902 on August 13. Perhaps this was intended as a correction for the duplication of 10 earlier numbers.

If, however, it is an error, I hope that your chagrin may be mitigated when I tell you that even "The Times" made several slips in its serial numbering in its early days.

In 1944, when the 50,000th number of "The Times' was in the offing, a survey was made to ensure that the issue receiving that number was in fact the 50,000th. It was found that the issue number 49,994 was in fact the 49,988th. Accordingly the next issue was numbered 49,994/2 and thereafter, during the two weeks ensuing each alternate issue was numbered in the same way. 49,995/2 and so on. Thus, on the great day, no pedant like myself was able to write and impugn the accuracy of the number of Number 50,000 – much more important matter than some may think.

Letters, R Isbister. Over the past two decades and more there has been a rash of so-called child psychologists deploring the use of corporal punishment in the rearing of children. Such people, with some of your correspondents, seem to base their arguments upon the assumption of an innate conscience despite lack of supporting evidence.

It seems more probable that any sense of right and wrong is acquired rather than congenital. From this basis, one can see the necessity for some sort of punishment and reward system to instill society's code of moral behaviour into children. It is not sufficient merely to indicate to a child the "errors of his ways" – such indications have value only when the child already has some moral sense and is able to perceive his actions as a contradiction to a logical extension of his existing morals.

It is in this process of morals acquisition that a form of punishment becomes necessary and for the duration of this process, in, ideally, decreasing amounts, the most efficient form of punishment is the infliction of physical pain as closely as possible sequential to the undesirable behavioural act.

This mode of punishment is psychologically less cruel than its alternatives: at least **one of the ideas promulgated by the medieval inquisitions** is not without merit.

Letters, Skinny Nurse. After seeing the photograph of the model of the nurse and airman figures to be added to the Cenotaph, I feel hurt. Consider, if you please, the size of the nurse's legs. Surely she would still stand upright if they were a little thinner.

I am sure the RSL would find, on survey, that a typical nurse, either 20 years ago or today, has better legs than the proposed bronze figure.

Letters, Long-Term Patient. Hospital patients would be appreciative if sister tutors could persuade the nurses they are training to cut their fingernails to just below the tips of the fingers. I have had many scratches from nurses' nails in the course of being sponged or moved about, and fingernails are a prime source of infection.

Fingernails grow quickly and need frequent cutting, but, it is well worth it, not only because short nails look young and pretty, but because of the benefit to the patient.

Letters, Laurie Mullens. It is saddening to reflect upon the apparent dearth of full-length mirrors in modern homes, as is suggested by the current fashion of above-the-knee skirts.

Apart from the unfortunate overall picture, surely there is nothing so unattractive as the human knee in action. Even when offered in the approved mannequin stance, there are so few knees worth looking at, anyway.

Letters, Robert Guille. I have long thought that a cable, carrying passenger cars, should be taken across the mile between North and South Head. Such a cable would help to ease traffic problems and would also provide Sydney with a tourist attraction unique in the world.

High above the sea, the view would be unparalleled and in no way would the cable detract from the natural beauty of the Harbour entrance. I have been informed by expert opinion that the suspending of a cable is quite possible and should present few difficulties.

Letters, A Mother. As the mother of a three-year-old epileptic child, who has had her questions about this illness answered repeatedly by specialists and general practitioners with "we will have to wait and see what develops – very little is known about epilepsy," I beg to disagree with Sir Macfarlane Burnet's statement that "**medical science has reached the stage when no socially significant improvement is possible.**"

In my child's case the cause of epilepsy is not known and in the doctors' words, "It may have been caused by any one of a number of things."

Surely to find all the causes of this heart-breaking illness and then eliminate it rather than dose the patient with drugs for the rest of his life would be a "socially significant improvement."

KEEP ONE EYE ON CUBA

It was obvious that something was brewing in Cuba. America and Russia were baring their chests at each other, and making growling noises. America was saying that the Russians were sending food and machinery and military equipment to Cuba. Russia was saying that America might claim that she had hegemony over that part of the world, and could control it, but that Russia did not accept that. Cuba was executing 100 men, allegedly sponsored by the US, who had plotted Castro's overthrow.

The result was that terse threatening messages were sent back and forth, the odd spotter plane was shot down, 150,000 American lads were dramatically called up to the military, and there were increasing suspicions that Russia were now sending ballistic missiles.

Still, Cuba continued to poke her tongue out at America, and was definitely clearing tracts of forest and building bases of some sort. Maybe these could be used for the housing and launching of missiles if she got some. The current situation was not at all clear, but it seemed certain that something big was on the agenda for all three countries.

SEPTEMBER NEWS ITEMS

Sydney's Blacktown Council has rejected fitting **safety belts** to Council vehicles. "The money can be put to better use."

The penny was starting to drop. The Federal Minister for Trade, Mr Crawford, in a speech today said that Australia must in future **sell wherever and whatever it could, to anywhere in the world**. There was no need to confine itself to the Empire.

Four aboriginal families will be brought from outback NSW to Sydney in an **"assimilation experiment."** The NSW Govt and the Aborigines Welfare Board will jointly do this. The families will get Housing Commission homes, and be helped with jobs. The aim is to show that they can live successfully in the modern community. **Hopefully**, they say, **the results will encourage more aborigines to make the move.**

Mid-September. The Heads of Commonwealth countries met with the British PM, McMillan, in Brussels. Collectively they said that **the situation over the Common Market looked "black"**, and that they feared that Britain would enter without adequate safeguards for the Empire. This was **the first time that they had so openly expressed such doubts**, and it was seen as an attack on the integrity of the British.

Sydney will get **double-decker trains** next September.

Twenty boy students were sent home from the Christian Brothers School, St Kilda yesterday **to change their shoes**. They had been told at the beginning of term that **pointed shoes** were not acceptable. The school now demanded that they wear "**more sensible ones**".

At the conclusion of the Commonwealth Heads of Government Conference in Brussels, British PM McMillan summed up the big occasion and told us they we would be OK and not to worry. **Britain would still look after us.**

Menzies returned to Oz with the message that, despite his **failure to gain anything definite at all from the Conference**, he had done a good job, and we were lucky to have him.

The Catholic Church was about to start its Second **Ecumenical Council.** Pope John XXIII convened this in the hope of **reviewing practices that might have outlived their time.** Over the next twenty years, a number of important reforms were made, and several of these were later negated. The end result is that now the Church is split somewhat between Conservatives, who like the old status quo, and Liberals who espouse changes. **An unhappy division.**

The NSW Government extended **Long Service Leave** to 1.5 million workers today. Workers will now qualify **after 15 years,** as opposed to 20 years previously. They will also be eligible **to pro-rata leave after 5 years,** rather then 10 years.

Lady De L'Isle, the wife of our Governor General, **died** after a long illness. Her body will be returned to England for burial. **The Governor General will continue in office**, and his family will continue to reside here.

At the end of the month, the US announced that it would re-introduce its naval blockade of Cuba along the same lines as before the Crisis. It would also continue with its fly-overs. **Business is back to normal.**

The Australian Cancer Society had **now accepted** British research that there is a definite **link between smoking and lung cancer.** It will join with the Oz Government in requesting tobacco manufacturers to **restrict glamour advertising** on their products. The manufacturers took no notice.

Early-birds were starting to point out the **so-called advantages** of **the decimal system** of currency, and weights and measures.

NASA physicist, Dr Robert Seitz, said that the **US would be able to send a 15-man expedition to Mars within 20 years**. The round trip would be of 100 million miles. Footnote: Fifty years later, it is safe to say that he was over-optimistic.

A writer to the *SMH* **said that 1972 is a multiple of 433.** He was wrong in that. He went on to claim that 433 is a multiple of 111. Not correct. He then claimed that, therefore, 1972 is regarded in New Guinea as a sacred number. How interesting.

THE AMERICA'S CUP

The America's Cup was a sailing trophy much valued in America. She had won it from England 110 years previously, and had held it ever since. About every four years, the yachting folk at America's Newport would hold heats to decide who could challenge them for the Cup, and then race against the leading contender in a series of seven races. In 1962, Australia had won its way into the final, and in September our *Gretel* was making a brave bid to wrest the Cup from America's grasp.

It was a strange fact that **this series of races had an enormous following in Oz. It was strange** because, **firstly,** yachting was not a particularly popular sport here. To play it, you needed some sort of expensive vessel and also a body of water nearby. Most Australians then could not manage both of these. **Secondly**, these boats were expensive, and carried crews of a dozen men, and dozens of support staff. **To sail in the Cup you needed to be filthy rich**, and there were certain elements in Oz who again did not qualify. This particular challenge, Australia's first, was funded by Sir Frank Packer.

In any case, the *SMH* wished Australia well with a somewhat jingoistic flourish. This attracted a very forceful rejoinder, and the Letters flowed freely after that.

Letters, K Peir. Your editorial "Appointment Off Rhode Island" takes a considerable amount for granted. Your conclusion about the cup challenge read "Every Australian today is wishing the challenger (Gretel) success." With due respect, I am a vigorous dissentient. On the contrary, I am one Australian who wants no such victory for this emblem of Australian egoism. In the last decade this country has wallowed in the hideous super-race philosophy and cult of the personality. There is a daily bombardment extolling the Australian virtues. Very little remains to which Australia does not lay the claim "we are the best in the world or we are equal to the best in the world."

The population is subjected to the nauseating sagas of Benaud in cricket, Verstak in California, or Laver and Smith in tennis. Providing Australia is the top-dog they are smiling, hand-waving warriors in anything, but oh, when they lose!

I am now assailed, assaulted and attacked – through ears and eyes – with the history of the famous yacht, Gretel, top, back, front, sides and middle, plus the broken boom. I get it for breakfast, lunch and dinner through newspapers, journals, television and radio. It's remarkable there are no roving mobile loudspeakers hooting "Gretel" into our faces at bus-stops or railway stations. Heaven preserve us if Australia wins!

And as for those patriots who propose to be alongside their radios around 2 a.m., I say jolly good luck to them. For mine it's all the luck to Weatherly – 4-0 I hope – over that very famous, famous yacht, Gretel.

Letters, A Ockerby. K M Peir deplores the fact that Australians claim "We are the best in the world, or equal to the best in the world." That is patriotism.

A similar spirit of patriotism has made the United States of America a great nation. Even in its early stages of development, the American believed that the United States was "God's own country" and that its products were superior to, and its sportsmen better than, any other nation's.

Sporting publicity is perhaps a little overdone in Australia, but success in any sport is entirely due to such publicity, together with the glamourising of its champions. The rising generation is thus stimulated to indulge in healthy sport, and in some it arouses an ambition to emulate the champions of today. The Australian Press, radio and TV mediums are fully aware of this and do what they can by way of promotion.

For heaven's sake do not let us have an inferiority complex with regard to our sportsmen. A superiority complex sets a standard to be maintained. If Gretel wins the America's Cup and proves that Australian technicians and boatbuilders are in world class, we can surely put up with the "ballyhoo."

Letters, J Barnett, Enmore. How refreshing to read Mr Peir's deprecation of the national preoccupation with sporting results, which in the last analysis don't matter one iota. To the non-Australian not conditioned to the chauvinistic, parochial partisanship engendered by the organs of propaganda, the set-up seems in the worst possible taste.

In regard to the super-race complex, I disagree. The confident person doesn't boast. Could it be that Australians, knowing that as yet their country is of small account, are pleading in the manner of the mother of an under-developed child: "Look! Isn't he bonny?"

Letters, A Davis, Pagewood. By all means let us hope that Weatherly wins the America's Cup, as K M Peir suggests. By all means wish that Benaud's side loses the Ashes by five to nothing. By all means let Rod Laver meet more than his match at tennis. In fact, let us change our character entirely and hope that the opposing side will win at every trial of strength. Then we will have nothing at all to throw our chests out about.

As it is, Australia has had good reason to be proud of its achievements in sport as in other activities – enough to make us feel a trifle cock-a-hoop, for like other people in this world, we are only human.

In any case, it is safe to say that, but for our achievements, Australia would be practically unknown by the outside world. As it is, our achievements have put us on the map so that we can meet other countries on even terms, whether it is on the field of sport or at the forum of the United Nations.

Comment. I suppose that some of you, not chastened by these hard words on patriotism, will still want to know whether we won the Cup or not. You will be pleased to know **we won the second race. But we lost the first and third. And then we lost the fourth**, by 26 seconds, the closest result in Cup history.

Then, finally **we lost the fifth** by a good margin. We were reportedly "valiant" in defeat. Races six and seven were not run since **the rubber was dead**.

COOKING PRAWNS AND LOBSTERS

I did my early schooling at a convent school and there I was taught by several nuns. Perhaps it was part of their own training, but I have clear memories of each of them talking at length about Saints Somebody-or-Other who were particularly kind to all living creatures. One of them, who always got a mention, was conspicuous because he supposedly was careful not to step on ants.

As I got older, I thought that probably his scrupulousness was exaggerated. But, as I read the following exchanges, I am inclined to re-consider.

Letters, Frances Vane. It is indeed good that voices are being raised in protest against depriving the sheep of their much-needed wool during the cold weather.

Another matter which has often arrested attention is the throwing of sea creatures into boiling water to kill them for food. That the Government permits such a practice is unbelievable.

Letters, G L Burgoyne. Frances Vane deplores the throwing of sea creatures into boiling water to kill them for food. Does she suggest they should be anaesthetised, or left to die before being eaten?

Letters, A Eather. Throwing crustaceans into boiling water is only one way of killing them. I can give the address of at least one suburban seafood shop where lobsters were seen alive and kicking in a display window. On making a complaint, a shop assistant explained that their customers were thus assured that the lobsters were fresh! The suffering involved in slowly dying in a shop window does not seem to concern anyone.

Letters, J McGrath. An article on the subject of killing shellfish by throwing them into boiling water appeared in the British Medical Journal 18 months ago.

It would seem that the most humane method is to put the creatures first into warm water, and then gradually heat it to boiling point. Thus the creature slides gradually into unconsciousness, and is probably the next best thing to being anaesthetised.

Letters, T Miles. Australia exports to the United States, annually, a huge number of crayfish tails. Is the public generally aware that the tails are torn from the crayfish while they are alive and the remainder of the maimed crustaceans left to die?

United States buyers require the tails in an uncooked state and Australian export (Fish) Regulations require, among other things, that the tails be placed under refrigeration within two hours from the time of killing. If tearing the tail from a live crayfish constitutes "killing," then millions of crayfish are killed in this manner in Australia annually.

Representations have been made to Commonwealth fishing authorities to have this inhuman practice stopped, but without result. Apparently no alternative method has been found practicable and the inoffensive crayfish must continue to die a lingering death.

Letters, T Atkinson. Crustaceans, I understand, have nerve centres and consequently feel pain more than do other forms of life.

The real cruelty to lobsters is by roasting them alive, which is done to a great extent in Europe and the United States, and to some extent in this country. I have been told that the lobsters writhe and scream and are tied by wire in front of the fire.

I took this up with the RSPCA in London many years ago, and was informed that there was little chance of doing anything about it. It is just a very cruel custom.

I have never eaten lobster and never intend to do so.

Letters, R Moore. Two years ago I saw a broadcast on English television that dealt with the cooking of crustaceans. Lobsters, it was explained, must be alive on entering the boiling water in order to give a perfect taste to the meat.

As many people objected to dropping a live lobster into boiling water, a professor of marine biology explained that it was possible to kill all sense of feeling in the lobster by piercing two nerve centres with a sharp instrument. This would satisfy both the gourmet and the lobster.

Letters, R Mayhew. The sympathy expressed towards crustaceans by "Herald" correspondents is misplaced and trivial. They are a class of invertebrates well down the scale of life and are related to barnacles, which are scraped off a ship's bottom without an anaesthetic!

It is fallacious to compare pain felt by man to that of animals as it is an irrefutable fact that pain is in direct proportion to brain power, in which the lobster is sadly lacking.

Letters, M Gaven. Current correspondence on the killing of crustaceans is to my mind most amusing. Surely it is of no consequence whether prawns feel pain when killed or not. If the thoughts expressed by correspondents were carried to their logical conclusion, should we not anaesthetise house-flies before spraying them?

Has T Bogue Atkinson, who deplores hearing that "lobsters writhe and scream," seen a fly rolling in pain and kicking its legs in agony after being poisoned with insecticide?

Letters, Joe Kreckler. Any man associated with the fish trade knows that the correct procedure for cooking lobsters is first to place them in a tub of cold, fresh water where they slowly drown. This prevents the loss of claws and legs, which, because of the lobsters' frantic struggles, become detached if the lobsters are placed direct into boiling water.

Comment. Once upon a time, back in the Good Old Days of 1962, a humble workman and his loving family, living the simple life, could go about their daily toil, scrimping and saving, but happy that every now and then, they would get some culinary feast that would compensate them for their daily penury. So that, perhaps twice a year, Dad would come home with a feed of lobsters, already cooked and cleaned, and all ready for the picking of the scrumptious white meat. The beauty of these creatures was that they were large, and half a lobster would do the average child, and a full one was more than most adults could eat.

Of course, that was all in the past. Now long forgotten. In 2021, lobsters have gone off the menu of humble workmen. The lobsters instead choose to be sent to Japan and America, and they get well compensated for the trip. Any that are too small for those exotic markets, the "kittens", are in fact on sale here, but are no bigger than Balmain bugs or Byron Bay bugs. Hardly worth the effort.

Of course, there's nothing I can do about it. Sometimes, when I see a kitten somewhere, I give an audible "humph". Most years, round about Easter, I go into a three-minute sulk. But neither of them help much. I'll just have to learn to live with it – but it's hard. Real hard.

A QUIET MONTH: GOOD FOR TRIVIA

Letters, J Groutsch. Photographs of the guard of honour that farewelled the King and Queen of Thailand at Kingsford Smith Airport on Friday show members of the First Battalion, Royal Australian Regiment, dressed like toy soldiers, complete with striped pants and pith helmets. Who would have recognised these men as some of Australia's front-line troops who have gained such an enviable reputation as fighting men in Korea and Malaya?

It is about time the Army authorities realised that there are no military uniforms more impressive or more soldierly than the Australian army's summer jungle greens or winter battle dress, with slouch hat. It is an insult to experienced troops to dress them up like toy soldiers or like candidates in some fancy-dress competition.

Letters, K Smith. The advent of television has meant that many of us have become familiar with the Red Army parading in Moscow, Trooping the Colour in London, or NATO troops in Europe. These parades are displays of strength and dignity. **In this country**, however, the Army appears to be confused as to whether its parades are displays of military strength or advertisements for a circus. It is just as likely that the march will be led by a pony, dog, donkey or whatever other animal is in vogue as a mascot. Nothing looks more ridiculous than soldiers striding along with an animal in tow.

The latest example of this kink in military thought was in the military guard of honour to farewell the King and Queen of Thailand. This was a ceremony to farewell a King, and a Shetland pony should have had no part in it. Had the animal disgraced itself at the wrong time, the embarrassment generally could have ruined the whole affair. Moreover, they are distractions which should never be permitted.

I would be interested to know whether any other nation participates in this childish behaviour.

Letters, Leslie Goodman. The suggestion by various motoring associations and advisory councils on the **compulsory fitting of safety belts** is a sad admission that the human race is incapable of safely handling the automobile. In effect, these governing bodies say, "Collisions are inevitable, so fit belts and hope you stay alive when the crash comes."

There is no denying that belts can save many lives. They will also encourage irresponsible drivers to take even greater risks. In support of compulsory belts, J M Last says it has been shown "that seat belts are particularly effective in accidents at speeds over 60 m.p.h." The fool who does over 60 m.p.h. needs a belt on the seat – good and hard. The speed limit in an unrestricted area is 50 m.p.h. and I have yet to hear a sensible reason for travelling any faster.

Only about 1 per cent of road "accidents" are accidents. The other 99 per cent are preventable collisions. Half a million people are killed on the roads each year, 2,000 of them in Australia. Not one country has solved the problem.

Australia can take the lead in preventing this senseless killing and maiming of valuable lives. The solution is simple: all that is necessary is to **multiply the penalties for careless and reckless driving by 10.** A driver would not think of overtaking on a bend or crest of a hill, or taking a corner so fast that the car rolls over, if he knew that his action could deprive him of a licence for five years.

Three months' suspension of a licence for the driver responsible for a slight collision and up to seven years' cancellation for a collision resulting in death would make us a nation of collision-free drivers within one month.

Just imagine, 2,000 lives saved every year, empty beds in hospitals, car insurance premiums down to 10/- . With no safety belts.

Letters, Spike Milligan, Woy Woy. En route to Sydney from the United Kingdom, I ventured ashore at Melbourne and there I bought from a mission aboriginal art shop a "guaranteed genuine aboriginal painting" from Crocodile Island. I was thrilled. Not so thrilled when visiting the official Missionary Society art shop, I saw the self-same painting, a conveyer-belt replica, as coming from an entirely different place. I also saw genuine conch shells painted by genuine aborigines using genuine plastic household paint.

At an art gallery I bought a painting with the solemn label, "A deeply sacred painting of the Raratjingo tribe." Since then I have discovered it is no such thing.

All this is disgraceful. Aboriginal art and religion are being debased for the sake of monetary gain. Missionaries should realise there is no such thing as an aboriginal who does not believe in God; as such the aboriginal is a religious person. Come home, missionary! The city of Sydney has more godless people than the entire aboriginal race.

Letters, Owen N Naylor. Some people, such as J Groutsch, always seem to have something to complain about! He objects to formal uniforms for soldiers on formal occasions, while K Smith doesn't like Shetland ponies in case they disgrace themselves.

Mounted police, when they perform traffic duty in the city streets, wear a working uniform. On formal occasions their dress adds to the pageantry of any parade. But in order to please J Groutsch we should ask them to wear their working uniforms at all times – and to make sure that K Smith is not shocked, they had better leave their horses at the barracks and proceed on foot!

JAPANESE WAR WAIFS

At the end of the War, Japan was devastated. Her major cities had been thoroughly destroyed, and her economy was in tatters. A Peace Keeping Force from the United Nations was considered desirable, and Australia committed a fair number of military to that. So that for about ten years, we had our soldiers living and breeding there, and the result was that when they then left, a number of small children were left without fathers.

Now, the issue was stirred up by a clergyman who said that Australia should accept responsibility for these unfortunate children.

Letters, V Law. The Rev H Perkins is reported as stating that the Australian Government and people should provide resources for Japanese waifs whose fathers were Australian Servicemen.

One. Does Mr Perkins wish to apply the same principles to similar children in the United Kingdom and the Middle East, or only to those in the countries of our former enemies?

Two. Does Mr Perkins intend to carry his submissions to their logical conclusion and request the US Government and people to provide resources to **aid the many Australian children whose mothers were abandoned by American Servicemen?**

Letters, Victor Segal. Approaches were made by the Benevolent Society to Mr Downer, Minister for Immigration, with a request that he grant the then president, Mr W Charlton, and myself an interview. Mr Downer wrote from Adelaide that he considered this unnecessary as this matter had been discussed at 'the highest Cabinet level" and it had been decided **that no action could be taken** (this in spite of the definite offers of adoption and offers to finance all expenses).

The matter was raised in Parliament, and the same answer given, and Mr Menzies also took an equally adamant attitude. Unsympathetic statements were made publicly by several prominent people here, even churchmen, and no co-operation could be obtained from any of the leading ex-Servicemen's and other organisations; in many cases, actual hostility was encountered.

I established an organization of prominent Japanese and Europeans in Japan, who obtained statistical figures, photographs, names, etc, and all other necessary information, which I offered to Mr Downer. In view of the Government's attitude, and in spite of the co-operation of the press, etc, it seemed hopeless to continue the task, which was regretfully abandoned. The position has become aggravated now by the increased ages of these children, who have suffered great humiliation and privation in the intervening years.

Letters, Alan Kitson. Australians are at least partially responsible for the fact that these children are illegitimate, ignored and of mixed blood, and surely something could be done to aid their material well-being and, if it is not too late, their education and opportunities in life.

This would hardly replace the normal family life that they have been denied – nothing can. It would, however, show that the "land of their fathers" has some feelings of compassion and it is, in my opinion, the minimum that we can do, unless, of course, we regard women as simply a natural portion of the spoils accruing to the victors, and as for the resultant children, well – "I'm all right, Jack!"

Comment. It turns out that nothing much was ever done. If the waifs had been from a nation that fought **on our side** during the War, there might have been a slim chance. But for the Japanese, our growing sense of tolerance had not yet extended that far. No Government action of substance eventuated, and there was no groundswell of public opinion for intervention.

OCTOBER NEWS ITEMS

Oxford in the US is currently the centre of vicious **race-riots** caused by the enrolment of a negro student at the **University of Mississippi there.** Yesterday, **two students were killed and 76 injured in the melees.** 14,000 troops were there then, and they have been re-inforced today by several plane-loads of parachutists.

Rev Alan Walker. "If there are **people on other planets** capable of communing with God, then **vast new mission fields** might open to the Christian Church."

Comodweal. This small town on the Qld-NT border was rocked this week by the **poisoning of 25 of its dogs.** All were household pets or working dogs. A town meeting came up with 125 Pounds to be offered as a reward for the conviction of the poisoner.

Sydney City Council at its next meeting will discuss extending **parking metres and tow-away zones** into the inner suburbs.

Cuba was still on the US black list. The US had just passed regulations that said **any country who traded with Cuba would be denied access to US ports.**

Cuba's Castro was also stirring the pot. He proclaimed that Cuba would never forsake **his Russian Communist allies**, and revealed that there were a number of **Russian technologists** already working in Cuba.

The English cricket team, led by Ted Dexter, arrived for a tour of Australia this week. When they arrived in Perth, the Oz Press immediately started to criticise the team. Apparently, six of the players **had developed a paunch** on the long boat trip across, and were classed as unfit. "They would rather lean on a bat than swing it." Such a welcome guaranteed that the tour would get off to a good start, and tradition would be upheld.

Last year, in 1961, the US unofficially tried to invade Cuba. A group of a few thousand mercenaries landed at the Bay of Pigs, and hoped the people of Cuba would rise up with them and overthrow Castro. **The venture was a complete failure,** and the US was acutely embarassed. 1,113 invaders were captured. **Castro was now demanding 62 million Dollars** for their release, and the US was dragging its feet in paying. More niggle and counter-niggle.

The Federal Government announced that **hospital care for all pensioners will be free.**

Letter from FAIRGO, Rockdale. The 11,625 boys and girls quoted in the *Herald* as **still seeking jobs** would not be unemployed for long **if selfish "retired" persons** occupying casual or permanent positions **surrendered them in favour of youth.**

42 yachts have entered for **this year's Sydney to Hobart Yacht Race.**

MURDERER ROBERT TAIT

Tait was a 41-year-old man who had raped and murdered a Melbourne woman in 1961, and who had been convicted of murder and sentenced to death. The decision on his guilt was clean cut, and undisputed. He had made various appeals to progressively higher Courts, and these had all been refused. Thus, the pronounced death sentence was due to be carried out in November. Most other States had basically decided that the death penalty would not be used again for murder, but Victoria was one State that was still posturing as "tough on crime." Therefore, the Victorian Cabinet insisted on the death penalty being carried out.

As the date of execution grew closer, agitation grew among students, clergymen, lawyers and others, to have the death penalty remitted. But the Cabinet stood firm. At this stage, the new plea of insanity was argued for the first time, and this muddied the waters.

The correspondence below follows the story as it moved along.

Letters, R Sinclair-Smith. The Victorian Government's decision not to commute Tait's death sentence has, in my mind, raised an emotional storm in the Melbourne Press that is hard to understand, and the demonstration by the Melbourne University students is surely nothing short of mass hysteria; their behaviour while the Victorian Premier was opening a new teachers' college was irresponsible and ineffective in a broad sense of the issue involved.

The appreciation of Tait's degree of sanity by eminent psychiatrists makes interesting reading.

Irrespective of the views of the Victorian Anti-hanging Committee, surely the emotional clamour to prevent Tait's hanging should be equated against the taking of an elderly lady's life at the Hawthorn Anglican vicarage.

Crimes of passion, hatred and even anger are understandable in some cases, but nevertheless unforgivable, but the crime this man committed against a defenceless, elderly woman who befriended him was diabolical, and in my mind hanging is too good for him.

While the consultant psychiatrist to the NSW Department of Justice has been reported as stating that records showed capital punishment was no deterrent to murder, this case is such that Tait should be made to pay with his own life for the life he took.

Letters, Peter Gillett. Unlike R C Sinclair-Smith, I profoundly admire the actions of Melbourne University students in the Robert Tait affair, and suggest that they are indicative of a moral awareness far in advance of that of their elders who comprise the Victorian government.

I would, of course, like to think that all these young people agreed with me and thought that capital punishment was always morally wrong. What in any event they do perceive and protest against is the hypocrisy of an officially Christian society carrying out an obviously unchristian act. By "unchristian" I mean cruelly retributive and blindly faithless.

Letters, E Emmerson. A photo of Melbourne University students demonstrating against capital punishment, published in the Press, showed one of their placards urging the abolition of hanging and, near it, another of their placards urging the hanging of Mr Bolte.

This remarkable piece of self-contradiction is indicative of the schizophrenic tendencies behind much of the shrill clamour now being raised against capital punishment.

This sort of thing, together with the irrational nonsense of the kind uttered at last Sunday's meeting called by the Sydney Central Methodist Mission to protest against capital punishment, can only increase public support for capital punishment.

Letters, (Mrs) Lorna Krone. Mr Bolte is to be admired for his determination to have the murderer Tait hanged.

We, the general public, are inclined to jump to conclusions and do not often know the true facts of murder cases. Only Judges and perhaps some members of the Police Force know the true story.

Life is supposed to be sacred, but that of the poor victim wasn't.

Letters, M Bearlin. The Rev H Guinness distinguishes between the principles underlying personal and judicial action as taught in the New Testament, but how can there be such an apparent discontinuity between love and justice in a democracy, where all men have the personal responsibility of framing the laws of justice?

Part of the problem in this discussion on capital punishment seems to be confusion about the meaning of "love." To love in the Christian sense is not to have a warm feeling around the heart, as previous correspondents have suggested, but rather it is a deliberate act of the will. To love a person is to have "an active concern for their life and growth." This involves taking personal responsibility for what happens to that person whether it be Robert Tait or the collection of persons we call society.

To have a concern for the life and growth of Tait is surely not to execute him, nor to release him. To have a similar concern for society is again probably never to release Tait, and also not to execute him. For we certainly miss the point if we think that the only person we might harm in executing Tait is Tait himself – we are in fact harming ourselves. For any society built on a concept less than that of love as defined will be stunted and not fully alive.

Comment. Action committees, against the hanging of Tait, were urgently stopping the execution by appealing to various Courts. In most cases, they were hanging their hats on the suggested insanity of the man at the time of the murder. These Courts got in the way of each other, and this meant that Tait's death was postponed four times in quick succession. In the long run, this factor weighed heavily on the Cabinet, and they commuted Tait's sentence to one of life imprisonment on November 7th.

CONTRACEPTION AGAIN.

I will make one more brief foray into this territory, because the arguments had now moved away from the dangers of usage, to other considerations that are worth covering.

Letters, Country-Woman. J F has reason to feel annoyed at the inconvenience caused her by chemists who, because of their religious beliefs, will not stock contraceptives.

However, in a big city there are always alternative sources of supply; this is not the case in many small country towns where there is often only one chemist and contraceptives are obtainable only by mail order.

An even more unfair situation arises when the Government medical officer is a Roman Catholic. In small country towns he is given the right to private practice and is often the only doctor within, literally, hundreds of miles. But these men refuse to advise patients on questions of contraception.

What right have they to accept positions in the Government service of a country which has no established religion, and then attempt to force their beliefs and practices on people of a different persuasion?

Letters, J Hopson. In reply to Mrs Eileen O'Halloran, may I, as a member of the "large denomination" referred to (Catholics), emphatically deny the insinuations and slurs she casts upon my "denomination." None of her statements, except that regarding the use of contraceptives, is true.

Mrs O'Halloran made use of the word "lust" in her letter. May I pose to her a simple question: Who are the more lustful: those who use the marital act as intended by the Creator and accept its obvious limitations and attendant responsibilities, or those who, refusing to accept the full responsibility of their actions and guarded by contraceptives, use their marital rights to indulge in sexual intercourse, ad libidum, ad infinitum?

Letters, Bridget S Gilling.   Lust, or, more moderately, sex attraction, shorn of mumbo-jumbo, is evidently a device to ensure the continuation of the race. So is an appetite for food; but few people would consider it desirable that we should eat only to live.

Whether divinely endowed or evolved from the primeval slime, the human ability to enjoy food and sex is there to be used, within reason and moderation. Contraceptives, therefore, are a defence against the real sin – the production of unwanted children, who will never have a place in the sun.

Letters, Winifred Wilcox.   Why the current discussion concerning the use of contraceptives? Woman's desire for sexual satisfaction is at least as strong as her mate's whatever some women may find it fashionable to pretend.

Neither the anguish caused by sexual frustration nor the mental exhaustion resultant from rearing conscientiously a large family is heaven-sent. It is Christian to "love one another." How loved and wanted children must feel when they realise, as they grow older, that their parents, who normally practice contraception, deliberately created them as a living sign of a truly happy union, rather than feeling that they are one of five or six unavoidable consequences.

THE CUBAN CRISIS

Comment. In writing up this event, I want to again make it clear that **I am getting my facts from Australian daily newspapers at the time.** These of course were loaded with all the propaganda that came from our alliances with America, and also reflected the distaste that all the Editors felt for Communism. I hope I have extracted the facts without too much of that propaganda coming through.

THE CRISIS ITSELF

In the last week of October, the situation in Cuba boiled over, and turned into the **biggest threat to peace that the world has seen since WWII, either before or since.**

The world first became aware that trouble was brewing when on October 23, President Kennedy announced that he would be addressing the nation on a most serious matter the following evening. No details were given, but it was clear that everyone should listen.

His subsequent statement said that the Russians were shipping large quantities of war materials, including nuclear arms, to Cuba, that a fleet of perhaps 40 ships was currently involved, and that this represented a threat to the safety of the US. He pointed out that the Russians were already in Cuba making bases for the launching of nuclear missiles that he expected were to be directed against America.

He announced that the US had established a ring of 150 vessels off the coast, and was imposing a blockade on the Soviet fleet. Any vessel that approached would be subject to search for offensive materials. If it refused to be search, it would be sunk. If it contained such material, and would not turn round, it would be directed to a US mainland port. If it refused to go, it would be sunk. President Kennedy pointed out the Russian fleet was now within two days' sailing of the blockade, and that this was a crisis of the greatest magnitude.

Indeed it was. On the face of it, the sinking or capture of Russian ships would almost certainly bring **about war between the two nations,** and that war, in the present circumstances, would **most likely be a nuclear one. The World was suddenly staring down the barrel of a real nuclear war**. For years, the sceptics, **including myself,** had been scoffing at the prospect. "Rubbish. Everyone knows such an event would destroy the entire world. No one would be stupid enough to start such a self-destroying event". Well, here was the world, two days away from the brink, and it remained to be seen if the management of the two nations would in fact be stupid enough to push on and actually let the rockets start flying.

Now I have to say, I have cribbed a little into the material that has been released since the crisis. I can point out that for these two days, American and Russian forces were on full military alert, and hundred and hundreds of missiles were primed, pointed, and ready to go. This was no dummy run. Frighteningly, there was a large number of senior advisers to both Kennedy and Krushchev (Mr K) who were advising that their own nation should strike the first blow. They wanted war.

Within the US, and the entire world, the crisis mounted as the ships came nearer. The first Russian ship, not part of the convoy, was allowed through. The second, actually the first of the convoy, was searched and released. The US, watching on TV emanating from satellites, held its breath.

In the meantime, Kennedy and Mr K had at last started to use the Red Phone. They were trying to communicate. It seems that, because of language barriers and transmission difficulties, they misunderstood each other a lot. But in any case, somehow, the message got through to Mr K that the Americans would indeed be prepared to start a war over this matter, so he ordered the offensive ships to turn round. This they did. Mr K in return extracted a promise from Kennedy that the US would not invade Cuba, an action that had already unofficially started. The invasion was cancelled.

As the Russian fleet turned round, Mr K ordered that the missiles already in Cuba be crated and returned. This was done over the next few weeks. Over the last few days of October, Kennedy made conciliatory speeches that said that both sides had learned from the incident, and that there was greater need for communication on both sides to forestall such events in the future. The world stood down. The sceptics went on the offensive again. "Rubbish. We are all wiser now." And the Cold War went on its merry way.

Comment. Who was the goody in all this.? The mobs that were rioting and demonstrating all round the world clearly thought America was the baddie. Or, in fact, did they think at all, or was this just another excuse to voice anti-Americanism?

In any case, they might have thought that every nation has the right to arm herself with any material she wants to. All nations elsewhere could do this: why not Cuba?

America replied that in period of WWI, she had declared the Monroe Doctrine that said, in effect, that the US was the custodian of all that part of the hemisphere, so that North and South America were hers to command in at least defence matters. So, she said, she could stop Cuba from getting nuclear weapons.

Russia argued that this was scarcely just. After all, the US had enormous nuclear destructive power concentrated on the Russo-Turkey border, all pointed at specific cities in Russia. The Russians had to live with this. Suppose Cuba installed US-pointing rockets on the US border. Why wouldn't the US live with that also? Because, replied the Americans, we are protected by the Monroe Doctrine. We don't have to.

Castro in Cuba had little say in the final decision. He had wanted the missiles to provide some balance of power. The US was putting a blockade on shipping coming to Cuba. It could do this because it had all the military power. If Castro could get missiles, he could get more control over his destiny, and perhaps bargain for a lifting of the blockade. In the long run, all he got was a promise that America would not invade his country. Not what he had hoped for.

So who were the goodies and baddies? Take your pick.

COLOURED IMMIGRANTS

I mentioned earlier that opposition to the White Australia Policy was starting to wane at a faster rate. But I would like to remind you that there were some quite sensible people out there who could put a good **argument** against relaxing the Policy.

Letters, Margaret Stowell, Headlands, Southern Rhodesia. News has reached us in Southern Rhodesia from Canberra that the Australian Junior Chamber of Commerce has decided to ask the Federal Government to relax immigration policy and encourage the entry of non-white immigrants to Australia.

While I sympathise with the moral principles behind such a move, I should like to point out that moral principles in this case may eventually cause a lack of moral principles should this relaxation of immigration policies take place.

Australia is one of the few countries of the world which does not have a racial problem – simply because Australia has encouraged the building up of a population of one race.

Having lived in southern Africa for the past five years and being face to face every day with racial strife, politically inspired though it may be, I always feel grateful for the Australian policy of immigration, in the hope that one day I shall be able to return to my homeland – a homeland completely free of racial problems.

Surely a lesson can be taken from the many other countries of the world where upheaval of the established order is taking place, where sections of the population suffer, through no fault of their own, an insecure future and the possible loss of the hard work and effort of previous generations in building up a heritage in homes, businesses and farms.

Even England has had to restrict her immigration policies – she has found that the continuous influx of other races is not proceeding smoothly as she had hoped – instead there have been riots, upsets and much emotional disturbance.

East is east and west is west and never the twain shall meet has more poignant meaning today than ever before, and I charge Australians to think long and wisely – to study the experience of other countries before taking irrevocable steps which will alter the Australian way of life, a much cherished thing, and much more appreciated when seen from the other side of the world.

NOVEMBER NEWS ITEMS

Film star and actor **Alan Ladd shot himself at the weekend**. He was cleaning a gun when it went off accidentally and shot him in the shoulder. **Nothing serious** for such **a tough guy**.

Drinking for natives in hotels was legal for the first time in New Guinea yesterday. All three hotels in Port Moresby were packed out with bare-foot natives, who drank "vast quantities" of grog. No serious incidents of violence were reported.

A prominent headline in a newspaper read "**EVEN STEVENS FIT.**" It turns out that Even Stevens is a horse, and it was ready for the **Melbourne Cup today.**

Frustrated shopper asks "What has happened to the **brown-paper bag?** It seems to me that anything heavier than a feather is too much for any size bag these days."

A Melbourne Cup radio commentator: "To use the phrase of **the classics.** He (Even Stevens) left him for dead."

A Press report from New Guinea. Some barmaids in some pubs in Port Moresby are complaining of stiff necks caused by craning over the counter to see that **all drinkers are shod**.

The Duke of Edinburough will extend his scheme to **allow Australians to qualify for his Award.** It will be presented to young people, up to 25 years of age, who perform well in a number of challenging but engaging activities.

Support for President Kennedy has grown markedly in the US since the Cuban Crisis.

Believe it or not, **the restoration of the GPO clock** in Sydney's Martin Place has started. When the NSW Govt promised to restore it some months ago, no one really thought they would actually do it. **Just goes to show you can't trust anyone.**

Last year, a deformed baby was born to a Dutch woman. It had no arms and disfigured feet, and had suffered because her mother had taken thalidomide during pregnancy. Her parents and family and doctor decided the child should not live, and after a few days gave it a barbiturate which killed the child....

Her mother this month **was tried for murder**. Given world publicity, she and the others were found not guilty. It had been feared by authorities that widespread rioting would have broken out if found guilty

The **Commonwealth Games** were soon to come to Perth. For the swimming events, a new 50-metre pool had been constructed. Now it was found that the **length of that pool was 50 metres. That is, in the centre.** But out at each edge it was **over two inches longer**. In sprints, many events were won by a touch. In the 1,650 yards event, the extra distance swum would total six feet. **Very embarrassing.**

DOCTORS AND COURTS

You will remember that doctors were earlier under some threat of being punished for not responding to calls to attend accidents. I can report that **no such legislation has been introduced**, and it is now certain than none will be.

Still, doctors lives were not at all beds of roses, as the following Letters point out.

Letters, H Greenberg. How many medical practitioners have been served with subpoenas at, say, 7p.m., to appear in court the following morning to give evidence in a case outstanding for perhaps two, three or even four years? How many of us have been called 10 or 15 miles to give evidence, only to be met with a bland smile from a solicitor's clerk – "that matter has been stood over"? How many of us have been expected to interrupt operation lists arranged weeks before, or leave our patients waiting in our rooms, unprovided for, to repeat trivial evidence which has already been supplied on statutory declaration or by certificate? And finally how many of us have failed in our efforts to collect witnesses' fees from the responsible solicitor?

Letters, R Else-Mitchell, Medico-Legal Society of NSW. Even if no comprehensive reform can be adopted, there seems no logical reason why the present rule that medical evidence must always be given orally in the witness-box should not be relaxed to allow detailed reports in a prescribed form, verified if necessary by affidavit, to be tendered as evidence without the consent of all parties being given. This would be conditional on copies of the reports having been previously supplied to the other party to the litigation a reasonable time before the hearing, a course which should be obligatory.

It is not being too optimistic to claim that if this simple step were taken it is probable that the attendance of doctors at court would, in the majority of cases, be quite unnecessary and there would be a consequent saving of Court time and expense which would be to the advantage of the parties and the community generally.

A FEW LETTERS ON THE CUBAN CRISIS

Letters, Irene Summy. The questions that we must answer, eventually, are these: Do we – or do we not – believe in and grant to every nation the right to choose her own weapons in her own defence, to select her own friends or enemies, to live her own way of life (whether it agrees with ours or not) and to decide which ships may visit her shores?

If one believes that Cuba has been – and has had reason to be – afraid of United States aggression (and remembering the Bay of Pigs blunder in 1961, who can deny it?) one cannot dispute her right to acquire weapons with which to defend herself. Even President Kennedy concedes this much.

Letters, Lakemba. Perspicacity seems not to be a guiding characteristic of President Kennedy's approach to the Cuban situation.

He speaks with dread of nuclear weapons being found in Cuba, as though this were the first time that he had realised their danger. He stands aghast at the thought of having to face these horror weapons.

But does not President Kennedy know that the whole world, for some time past, has been facing this situation, in all its seriousness, just as he is now? Cuba is, geographically, one small place, explosive enough at the moment, but the main concern of thinking people the world over is with this globe of ours that is plastered with nuclear devices which could, in the event of a mistake, spell annihilation.

The real problem is a world one, not merely Cuban, and the sooner East and West get together and put their humanitarian talk into practice the better.

SPARE THE ROD

Every teacher in the land wanted a nice quiet time with kids who would shut up, behave, and do their work. But sadly, this could not always be arranged, and the badly-behaved child needed somehow to be disciplined. The current situation, though it varied from State to State, was often that the classroom teacher could send the child outside, but could not use the cane. That came down to the headmaster or someone deputised by him. Girls were rarely caned.

In November, discussion of this topic was notched up by a letter from a chap called Samuel Marsden. I was delighted to know that the famous gentleman, presumed dead for about 200 years, was still alive and kicking.

Letters, "Samuel Marsden". Recently, at a metropolitan High school, my son and another lad were given two cuts of the cane for talking in class.

I am appalled that children have to risk serious damage to their fingers in this barbarous fashion. At the somewhat unenlightened GPS which I attended over 30 years ago, they knew better – they caned us on the buttocks where there was little or no danger of breaking bones.

Letters, L Champion. Instead of discussing the merits of caning children on the fingers or buttocks, "Sam Marsden," who takes the name of the hypocritical flogger-parson, should consider the appalling psychological effects of any type of corporal punishment not only on the victim but also on the person who inflicts it.

Although youngsters may laugh off this type of treatment, their subconscious minds do not laugh it off and their deep-seated resentment burns unceasingly for the rest of their lives. This resentment often turns them into floggers or advocates for flogging in their adult life – a psychological fact which every parent and teacher should never forget.

Letters, L White. The letters of "Sam Marsden" and "Rock Bottom" are fair samples of how the modern generation of youth is being pampered by fond parents. They are also a lot of sentimental drivel.

My school days ended in 1899. I can still well remember the very frequent "sixers" (three on each hand) and never thought otherwise than that they were well deserved, but I cannot recall having made any complaint to my parents. Had I done so, I feel sure – as I no doubt felt then – that I would have received little sympathy.

"Rock Bottom" says "goodness knows how many potential rheumatoid arthritics these men are unwittingly producing." It will be noted from the above that my fingers were not spared the rod. I am now approaching the age of 80, but no sings of rheumatoid arthritis have yet appeared.

The imaginative description of the human hand by "Rock Bottom" is worthy of a place in the "Herald's" "Sayings of The Week". If, however, two cuts with the cane can destroy or even damage this wonderful invention (who invented fingers?) one can imagine the damage to fingers which would be caused by even one day's hard work of an ordinary labourer.

It may be that the bones of the fingers of modern youth are made of chalk, in which case these complaints might be justified.

Letters, R Morgan, Headmaster. It seems to me quite out of order that any child should be caned on the hands, but the fact that corporal punishment is sometimes necessary cannot be denied. A few smart strokes on the bottom are a splendid deterrent to naughty boys in an independent school.

Apart from the painful but certainly temporary nature of the punishment, the gross indignity suffered by the boy, who has either to clutch his ankles or the padding of his headmaster's armchair, does far more to prevent the recurrence of an offence than the caning itself.

While caning should be undertaken with care (for I remember when I was at school a master who was a poor shot once sliced a boy's ear), its good effect on the boy and on other boys, and **the general bonhomie felt by all** involved afterwards is of much benefit in the character-training of young lads.

Letters, L McGregor, Gladesville. L E Champion writes of the "appalling psychological effects of any type of corporal punishment" on children.

If his view is correct, it is a great wonder that we have had prominent men and women in our long history. In earlier days the father in the home was sometimes a minor tyrant, yet our great ones of music, literature, science and so forth have come from many such homes.

Today the teenager is a problem because he reads, and therefore knows, that he must not be physically punished for anything he does. Some of these young people end up in gaol, a punishment far worse and more prolonged than the old-fashioned and salutary birching over a stool.

Letters, M Rietsema. I have followed the recent correspondence on the caning of schoolchildren. As a migrant from Continental Europe I generally try to respect and understand the habits of the people of this country.

I am disgusted over this talk of how and where (what part of the body) caning should be applied. Every teacher who uses the cane deserves a solid hiding. Corporal punishment belongs, like hanging, to the Middle Ages and must be stopped in a community that considers itself advanced and enlightened.

It might also be noted that while caning exists in Australian schools the standard of Australian education is for once not equal to the best in the world.

Letters, T Delmere. In his condemnation of the caning of children, L E Champion is voicing the very attitude that has caused the blackboard jungles and teenage hooliganism in America – an attitude fostered by many (though not all) psychiatrists, psychologists, sociologists and the like.

However, it is somewhat hypocritical for the nation to approve of corporal punishment for children but not for hardened criminals. The answer is to approve of it for hardened criminals as well, not to disapprove of it for children.

Letter, T Griggs. Men get everything. Why can't girls get caned too?

Comment. I was educated in Catholic schools, and at the time, corporal punishment was liberally dispensed. In primary school, at a convent, the nuns started using **the ruler** in First Class, and my knuckles bore the brunt of that. In Fourth Class, **a cane** became the instrument of torture, and mass executions were the order of the day.

In High School, at a Marist Brothers School, my First Year Class had the sons of 78 pig farmers, pumpkin-pickers and coal-miners in it, so that mass canings were very much the in-thing. After Third Year, we became "Gentlemen", and the cane disappeared.

I think this was typical of Catholic education at the time. I remember well talking to State School students at the time, and it was true for them that canings were the prerogative of only the Headmaster.

I do not think that these punishments left much of a mark on me. You can probably tell from my above writing that I still carry some resentment, but I can take that or leave it. In fact, there was one caning of four full-blooded cuts that actually did me good, and I always been grateful for them.

In any case, the problem of school discipline still remains. Here we are in 2022, many years later, and the problem is probably greater that ever. I suspect that no matter what is tried, deviance is part of the human herd, and try though we may, it will keep turning up.

BREAD FROM SEAWEED.

Here is the topic that I know many of you have been waiting for.

Letters, E Jones. It seems almost incredible to me that Laver "bread", which is sold in great quantities on the Swansea market in Wales – quantities restricted only by the amount of seaweed taken from the sea and from which it is made – has not found its way to Australia or is not made here.

Laver "bread' is made of a dark green seaweed into little mounds like a bun and is quite soft. Cooked with bacon or ham, it makes a delicious meal. There is a fortune awaiting any person or firm that will take up its manufacture.

I have not the least doubt but that there is a tremendous amount of the same seaweed around our coasts. I have picked up a bit of dark green seaweed in Long Bay and it tasted to me like the seaweed that is used in Wales in manufacturing Laver "bread."

Letters, B Rees. Many Welsh families in Sydney and the South Coast do collect the weed and make their own bara lawr. In the Sydney area, Welsh settlers, nostalgic for Welsh food dishes, collect the seaweed from the northern beaches. Some Welsh bara lawr cookery experts have told me that not all Australian seaweed is suitable for the making of seaweed bread, only that collected in certain areas of the South coast and a part of the northern beaches.

Welsh food, though not as attractive and tempting to the eyes as Continental dishes, is among the most nutritious in the world. Like their culture, the Welsh keep it mostly to themselves. I have been collecting Welsh recipes for the past two years, and I have learnt that most of the recipes have been stored away in the memories of mothers and daughters over the centuries.

Incidentally, during recent research into Welsh culinary tastes, I learnt that even the famous French cooking owed its beginnings to the lavish food preparations and hospitality of the Welsh princes and lords of six and seven centuries ago. It appears that French noblemen used to travel to Wales to seek their brides because they were "noted for their beauty, queenly carriage, excelling in their cooking and tables."

Letters, The Entrance. Over 50 years ago, while visiting the islands of the west of Scotland and on the coast of north Scotland, I helped to gather a seaweed called dulse. This seaweed is of the "ribbon" type, of various lengths and about two inches wide. It was gathered on the rocks at low tide and washed several times in fresh water to remove salt. It was then spread on white cotton sheets and allowed to dry in the sun. When dry it was crisp.

A small quantity placed in a saucepan with milk added and allowed to simmer gently for a short time sets like a junket after it has been poured into a bowl through a strainer and allowed to cool. It is served with fruit, etc, and has a very high food value and was considered a delicacy. In Ireland it is known as Irish moss and apparently in Wales it is known as laver.

The definition of dulse, Irish moss and laver will be found in any standard dictionary.

Letters, Don Robertson. The thought of hordes of nostalgic Welshmen descending on our fishing spots to harvest their weed has struck terror into the hearts of this gallant band of sportsmen. Ulva lactuca, or rock cabbage, is the staple diet of the blackfish and drummer. These two noble fish provide the main sort for hundred of courageous "rock hoppers," who, armed only with a slender rod, a line of cobweb dimension and a delicate leaf of rock cabbage, spend their leisure time attempting to lure the wily fish from their underwater hiding places.

Lest our weedbeds be laid bare could you please publish a recipe for old-fashioned English bread that uses flour as a base? This formula is apparently unknown to our master bakers.

TOUGH TIMES FOR ANIMALS.

The condemnation of the brumby cull was widespread. How did people feel about bull-fights? We have a few people who were happy to tell us.

Letters, R Roberts. Senora Dolores Comas, of the World Federation of Animal Welfare Societies, advised Australian tourists who plan to visit Spain not to attend the bullfights. Well let us reciprocate and advise Spanish tourists and any other tourists not to attend our race meetings, trots or greyhound racing when visiting Australia.

In any sport where animals participate, there is always a certain amount of cruelty. People accept it and enjoy the sport for what it is. Bullfighting is no exception and el toro, instead of being slaughtered in some abattoir, dies amid a blaze of glory and fanfare.

The skill and courage of the toreadors, matadors, and picadors must be admired by all who attend the bullfight. What an art! Not to mention the grand parade before the fight, all in traditional costumes, and the arena itself, historical and colourful, is an education to any tourist. It is Spain itself. **Ole to the bullfights in Spain and let us see a few in Australia.**

Letters, Elizabeth Vitek. Rhoda Roberts seems to have her facts a little confused. Australian racehorses quite frequently survive to race on future occasions. The bull in the bullring is denied the opportunity to fight again. And how could a bull appreciate the difference between dying quickly and humanely in an abattoir and being tormented to death in a bullring, blaze of glory, fanfare and all?

This ritual slaughter cannot be called sport, and I am quite sure that we do not want it here in Australia.

BRITISH ATTITUDE TO SPORT

Letters, John A Lister, Turramurra. I feel I must comment on the statement by Stuart Mackenzie that "the British attitude of being perfect gentlemen in sport is stupid and old-fashioned," and "a success-at-all-costs attitude is badly needed in Britain."

If their attitude is old-fashioned, then long may it continue, as a lesson to the rest of the world. **Every Englishman would rather have as his epitaph "he was a sportsman and a gentleman" than "he always won."**

As an Anglo-Australian, I refuse to believe that the average Aussie supports Mr Mackenzie's view.

PLATYPUSES GALORE

Back in 1962, if I had come across some fauna that was rare, and if perhaps I thought that its habitat was in danger, I might have thought about giving it to the Zoo. Well, that's what happened to three platypuses, and you will see what followed.

Letters, N Haseler. It is now more than a month since an outcry arose over the action of two men in capturing three platypuses and sending them to Taronga Park.

According to the "Herald," the Fauna Protection Panel was to consider the matter as far back as October 11. Surely, then, it is high time that the community was informed what has developed in this important case. The Fauna Protection Panel being an official body, the public has a right to know what, if anything, it has done to enforce its vaunted safeguarding of "rare fauna," and, of course, the same point applies to the responsible Minister.

Some two years ago, when a number of young jabirus were taken from a nest and sent to Taronga Park, the Chief Secretary, Mr Kelly, stated that the zoo had no more right than any private person to receive protected fauna. Obviously, the zoo authorities have disregarded that declaration, and so it will be interesting to know the Minister's intentions in the present case in regard to both the captors and the receivers. I suggest, too, that many people would like to learn whether any of those unfortunate platypuses are still alive.

Letters, Ruth Schleicher. For the benefit of Haseler and others who are interested in the case of the three platypuses, perhaps you could publish the following information:

We have now received a letter from the Chief Secretary stating that approval has been given for the institution of proceedings against the person who captured the animals and that the matter of the Taronga Park Trust's receiving protected fauna without the necessary prior approval is being taken up with the trust by the Fauna Protection Panel.

So it would seem that the widespread protests by nature-lovers over these illegal proceedings have had some effect.

THE MELBOURNE CUP

Letters, G Perkins. Once again the community has been treated to the spectacle of a nation's work coming to a halt, not because of a legitimate holiday, but because of a horse race – the Melbourne Cup.

Within the last month in this country we have seen an international crisis, with the world poised on the edge of nuclear war, pass almost without comment by the man in the street. We also saw brutal murder denied its just deserts in accordance with the opinion of a large section of the community opposed to capital punishment.

Then, finally, we have witnessed hundreds of thousands of precious pounds changing hands through sweeps and bets on a horse race.

How can the members of a nation, whether Liberal, Labour or Communist, Christian or non-Christian, possibly justify their indulgence in this annual orgy of gambling given that there are thousands of children and adults living in poverty and starvation in various parts of the world?

Even the pupils of church schools are today corrupted by this annual betting spree, thereby acquiring the taste for gambling. Surely there is something radically wrong with this Christian nation's sense of moral values, and ideas of what is important and unimportant.

DECEMBER NEWS ITEMS

All **women gaol prisoners** will go through a **reformatory** opened yesterday, the NSW Government announced. Inmates should regard it as **a school**, and they will be taught hair-dressing, beauty care, and dress-making. They will be encouraged **to take part in academic studies** in the arts and sciences.

The Minister for Justice in NSW: that there were **100 women prisoners in NSW**, out of a total prison population of 3,100.

Rents for dwellings were fixed in about 1941. Since then, in most States, landlords **have not been allowed to raise rents.** This was generally not considered fair to them. Unless you were a tenant. Now the Government is considering legislation that would enable tenants to **leave their tenancy rights to their children in their wills.**

The NSW Government gave approval for **petrol vending machines to remain open at all times.** This replaced regulations that restricted them to normal trading hours, and included no Sunday time.

A woman in Moora in WA gave birth to a child on Sunday. The doctors realised **that a twin was also due**, but because its birth might be complicated, she was shipped to Perth. There a second child was duly delivered. Thus **the twins were born 118 miles apart and a day apart.**

Nineteen **thalidomide babies** were born in NSW this year. Nine of them were born dead. The others were congenitally deformed.

American actor, **Charles Laughton**, aged 63, died **yesterday**. He will be remembered for his roles in **"Mutiny on the Bounty", and "The Hunchback of Notre Dame."**

Parents were **resisting the herding of children** into the Showground for **the Royal Visit** in March. Many wrote that, last time, children were on their feet for five hours, without water, in heat, and unable to move for hours. **They got a glimpse of the top of the Queen's head**.

A boxer, southpaw Geoff Dynevor, became **the first aboriginal to win a gold medal at the Commonwealth Games.**

Some pathetic words from **President Kennedy**: "I believe the moment may be at hand to initiate the beginning **of the end of the upward spiral of weapons competition.**"

A Sydney businessman, Vincent Labb, plans **to stage bull-fights in Sydney and elsewhere** on a regular basis. He already has 30 bulls lined up from Spain, and 10 leading matadors. He expects **crowds of 100,000** at the Sydney Showground....

A Chief Secretary's Department spokesman said he had no doubt that **the plan would be rejected.**

BRUTALITY TO BRUMBIES

At this time of year, the newspapers always fall into line with politicians, and present a world that is pleasant and sweet, with not so much violence and trauma and outrage as usual. But they could not hide the grim facts from the episode below, and they could not sidetrack the huge public response that was stirred up.

Letters, P Watson. We read that these wild creatures are to be hunted out of the ranges by aeroplanes, terrorised and kept moving towards the yards by jeep and motor cycle. Then their long and painful journey by road is to begin, followed by a minimum of two days crowded into stock trains between Bourke and Sydney. There they are to meet their destined end from these sufferings in potted pet food.

Somewhere there will be profit margins; otherwise these unwanted animals might have had their lives swiftly and mercifully ended without these additional cruelties.

In lodging this protest against these shocking practices it is hoped that the callous disregard of the suffering of stock when travelling long distances by rail may soon belong to the past in this country.

Letters, Colin Simpson. Newspaper reports of the proposed round-up of 4,000 or 10,000 (figures vary) wild horses in south-western Queensland for killing in Sydney for pet meat have left me sickened, angry and wondering whether Australia can be called a civilised country.

We can't expect to be regarded as civilised if we countenance this kind of cruelty. Cruelty negates civilization.   No public conscience about it, no status as a civilised people.   It's as simple as that, for us – but not for the horses.

Any horse, not fortunate enough to break a leg on this part of the death-haul and get shot at Bourke, is in for a 512-mile trucking from Bourke to Sydney. The shunt-bang-crack, over-packed haulage of cattle and sheep in Australia is demonstrably and notoriously cruel, anyway.   With wild horses it will be worse.   I can hear the "Sure, they got food and water," but can they get at it?   And, "Listen, mister, they gunna be pet food anyway, soon.   They gotta die, see?"   But how many times?

Letters, J W E. If we were, to analyse the human race, the characteristic which would stand out above all others would be man's cruelty.   In wartime it was his cruelty to his fellow man – the prison camps of the Japanese, the death camps of the Germans.   In peace it is cruelty to the poor dumb animals of the world.

All too often this comes under the guise of "sport" – the tiger-drive for the Queen in India a few years ago; the rounding-up of a stag for the Prince of Wales to slaughter in recent weeks.   We read of a South Australian man who goes shooting wombats by night "for sport" and we read of the Duke of Edinburgh shooting 1,500 game birds in four days of "sport" in Italy on his way home from the Games.

To most people "sport" is an affair where contestants meet on equal terms: a cricket match between sides of equal numbers, a tennis match between teams in the same grade. Logically, shooting should feature guns on both sides and if the hunted animal could fire back with an equal chance then, and then only, could it be classed as sport. Until then it should be called "butchery" and "slaughter" – it should not be allowed to foul the term "sport."

The occasions on which we humans really excel ourselves are those where the profit motive is allied to our natural cruelty. No doubt they will enjoy this little bit of "sport"-cum-business venture. They make me ashamed to admit to being a member of the human species.

CHRISTMAS ON US AGAIN

Every year, just before the New Year I get a great sense of relief when the great pagan festival of Christmas is over, and I can settle down again into my boring rut. The trouble is that it, Christmas, will not stay away, and it keeps coming back. Here it is again pressing on me for acknowledgement, and arguing that I could not possibly write a book such as this without any appropriate mention.

This year, instead of listing all the goodies that can be bought and distributed, I will limit myself to a single possibility. Also, normally I give preference to children's toys and other destructive things, and then to the fancy goods for women. This year, I will give men a go, but am cunning enough to include women as well. I am not a smoker myself, so I have no use at all for this gadget but it seems, nevertheless, that everyone should have one. Even for children, who to their delight, will find it easier to light bush fires in the school holidays.

Below, I have included **the newspaper spiel** for the product. Notice that the heading shown by me was the one **shown in the newspaper.**

CHRISTMAS SPECIAL FOR ALL THE FAMILY

For the new butane lighters are splendid value as gifts. For the ladies and the gentlemen, two pocket lighters: the streamlined Veraflame or the smaller, more conservative Victor. For the family gift, four table models: the Claridge, the Norseman, the Adelphi and, of course, the famous Queen Anne. In chrome, pigskin, black, lizard or Scandinavian wood finishes; ranging in price from ninety-six shillings to per filling (six to eight weeks for the pocket lighters, longer for the table models).

TIDYING UP DUTCH NEW GUINEA

The transition to Indonesian rule went smoothly. The UN had agreed to a number of procedures and rules, and the Indos had stuck to them. Since then, apart from incidents of no lasting consequence, everyone has behaved themselves. In particular, the Indos have made no grabs for east New Guinea territory, and they have not become a Communist satellite. None of the dire predictions have occurred.

TIDYING UP CUBA

The Russians withdrew all of their equipment and that process went well. On the other hand, Castro and the US went on with their lovers' tiffs. For example, immediately after the Crisis, Castro said he would send home some big Russian bombers and stop the fly-overs of US territory. The US said that they would stop the shipping blockade into Cuba by independent nations. It all sounded sensible, but it all took months of bargaining and reversals and, as you know, all of that has continued to the present day.

TIDYING UP STATE AID FOR SCHOOLS

Soon after the Goulburn incident, the Catholic Church and the NSW Government actually started to talk. Over a period of months, then years, State Aid was granted, and later became part of the Federal bag of tricks as well. It has grown to the stage where there are claims the private schools are getting too much aid, and that it is being wasted on swimming pools and ovals. The pendulum might have swung too far.

TIDYING UP THE COMMON MARKET

What a pain in the neck. It became obvious as the year progressed that Britain would enter the Market , and that there was little she could do to preserve Commonwealth preferences.

There were all sorts of die-hards here who said Britain would never desert us, and others who said that if she did enter the Market, it would be a calamity for Australia. But there was a growing body of opinion arguing that entry would not be such a bad thing, and that maybe we would be better off if we shed the protective mantle we had been hiding under, and went out into the real world and competed with all comers.

The end result was that Britain did enter, and that she did get some safeguards for us. But not many, and we were quickly forced to stand on our own two feet. As it turned out, this did not hurt the nation one bit, though there were many individual traders who bore the brunt of it.

In any case, today we stand quite ready to trade anywhere we can. Right now, our biggest trading partners are China, Japan and the US. Notice that Britain is not included. When you think about it, compared to the dominanceof Britain fifty years ago, that is a big change.

Some things do chsnge.

A CHRISTMAS MEMORY

Back in the mid-forties, I went to a regional city nearby and enjoyed the fun of the Chriustmas fair. The War was over, and all the restriction were off, so there was plenty to see and do.

A Merry-go-round of course. And dodgem cars, and laughing clowns, a bearded lady and a strong man. clairvoyant, a boxing troupe. Everything you could want, including a Ferris Wheel,

This vertical monstrosity was about 50 yards high, with bucket seats, to hold a pair of people, it spun round in a vertical circle, while all the young girls got their protective cuddles for their beaus.

But not from me. I was not adventurous, and was too young to want the embrace of any girl.. I was scared of the height, But I got all brave, and took a ride. I did not enjoy it all all. When it stopped, I went behind a tent, and was sick.

In 1972, there was another Christmas fair in a Showground near me. I looked at the Ferris Wheel, and thought I should give it another go. After all, I was a fully-

grown man. Forget your childish memories. Go for it....
So, I did.

I did not enjoy it at all. When it stopped, I went behind a tent, and was sick.

Some things do not change.

SUMMING UP 1962

In summing up 1962, I want to point out some things that we had going for us. Let me start with war. We didn't have any. We had no external war, no civil war, no troops going to foreign war. No lists of dead and maimed as in past years, no families terrified at the approach of the postman. No body bags. Just a peace that let us live our lives as wisely or foolishly as we chose.

Let me pass quickly through a number of other things we did not have. We did not have a shortage of food. There was an abundance of fruit and veggies, lots of meat, gallons of all fluids to drink. Granted some grumps complained because they could not get lobsters as freely as in the past, but these silly old buggers should count their blessings.

We had no plagues or famines or epidemics. No polio, no TB, no cholera. We had plenty of cheap clothing and woolen blankets. We had a big housing shortage, but nothing compared to Africa and Manila and South America. Anyone who tried could get a job, anyone who had a job could get a loan from a bank (after a while), and buy a car, and a lawn mower.

What I am trying to do in a few words is to point out that, compared to most other places, this nation was really well off. We did have many things to complain about. The sheer folly of our politicians, running round snapping at the heels of others. The perpetual fighting between States and the Commonwealth. The state of our roads, and our sewerage. There was never anything to watch on TV. But against these, and now talking social issues, aborigines and women were starting to advance their causes more rapidly. Commercially, we were doing alright. We could be better, and believe it or not, when the Brits cut our strings and joined the Common Market, we did pull our socks up, and after a few years were stronger than we would ever have been attached to Britain.

I could go on, but you get my point by now. 1962 was a golden year. I am happy to say that it was not at all unique among all the golden years that we had before and since, in this golden land of ours. I can remember years when things were not so good. Thirty years previous, we were in the doldrums of the Depression. Exactly 20 years back, things were as bleak as could be. In the Vietnam, **years later,** in the 1960's, the body bags did appear. There were bad years for us, in the past and in the future.

But I am happy to repeat, 1962 was one of the golden years. If you were born in that year, I suggest you should feel good about it, and celebrate your good fortune with a long cuddle with the people you love.

MORE INFORMATION ON THESE BOOKS

Over the past 16 years the author, Ron Williams, has written this series of books that present a social history of Australia in the post-war period. They cover the period from 1939 to 1973, with one book for each year. Thus there are 35 Titles in the series.

To capture the material for each book, the author, Ron Williams, worked his way through the Sydney Morning Herald and the Age/Argus day-by-day, and picked out the best stories, ideas and trivia. He then wrote them up into 180 pages of a year-book.

He writes in a direct conversational style, he has avoided statistics and charts, and has produced easily-read material that is entertaining, and instructive, and charming.

They are invaluable as gifts for birthdays, Christmas, and anniversaries, and for the oldies who are hard to buy for.

These books are available at all major retailers. They are listed also in all leading catalogues, including Title Page and Dymocks and Booktopia.

Over the nexr few pages, summaries of other books years from 1939 to 1973 in the Series are presented.

A synopsis of all books in the Series is available at:

www.boombooks.biz

****

THERE ARE 35 TITLES IN THIS SERIES
For the 35 years from 1939 to 1973

ABOUT THIS SERIES

.... But after that, I realised that I knew very little about these parents of mine. They had been born about the start of the Twentieth Century, and they died in 1970 and 1980. For their last 50 years, I was old enough to speak with a bit of sense.

I could have talked to them a lot about their lives. I could have found out about the times they lived in. But I did not. I know almost nothing about them really. Their courtship? Working in the pits? The

Lock-out in the Depression? Losing their second child? Being dusted as a miner? The shootings at Rothbury? My uncles killed in the War? Love on the dole? There were hundreds, thousands of questions that I would now like to ask them. But, alas, I can't. It's too late.

Thus, prompted by my guilt, I resolved to write these books. They describe happenings that affected people, real people. The whole series is, to coin a modern phrase, designed to push your buttons, to make you remember and wonder at things forgotten.

The books might just let nostalgia see the light of day, so that oldies and youngies will talk about the past and re-discover a heritage otherwise forgotten.